RUN
THE ALPS
SWITZERLAND
30 MUST-DO TRAIL RUNS

RUN
THE ALPS
SWITZERLAND
30 MUST-DO TRAIL RUNS

DOUG MAYER – KIM STROM – JANINE & DAN PATITUCCI

HELVETIQ

THANK YOU!

A big Thank You to the runners who joined us on these routes: Kirra Balmanno, Derek Strom, Joe Grant, Pascal Egli, Alister Bignell, Krissy Moehl, Brody Leven, and runners who provided their stories of running in the Alps: Diego Pazos, Julia Bleasdale, Martin Anthamatten, Lizzy Hawker.

The staff at 'Run the Alps' and Alpinehikers, Mike Ambrose, Maartje Bastings, Alain Bustin, Gil Caillet-Bois, Hillary Gerardi, Troy Haines, JeePee Lüthi, Gaetan Vanwynsberghe, Philippe and Sophie Zurkirchen.

We'd also like to thank the regional Tourism Offices for their generosity in supporting our visits.

Run the Alps Switzerland: 30 Must-Do Trail Runs
By: Doug Mayer, Kim Strom, Janine & Dan Patitucci

ISBN: 978-2-940481-47-7

Published by Helvetiq
Graphic Design & Layout: Lucas Guidetti Perez, Timothy Hall
Cover: Timothy Hall
Proofreading: Aaron Wyckoff
First Edition: May 2018
Printed in the Czech Republic

Legal Deposit
May 2018
Swiss National Library, Bern

'Run the Alps' is a registered trademark of Run the Alps LLC and is used with permission.
www.runthealps.com

For Ueli

And the sun is setting.
The sun will rise another day.

— Eddie Vedder

CONTENTS

TRAIL MAP

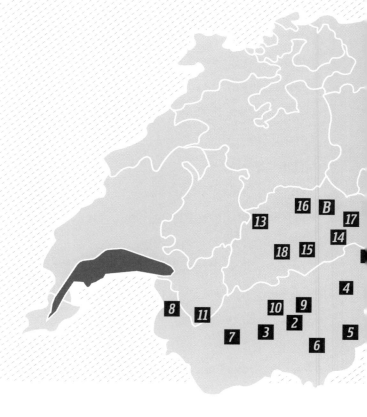

VALAIS

BERNESE OBERLAND

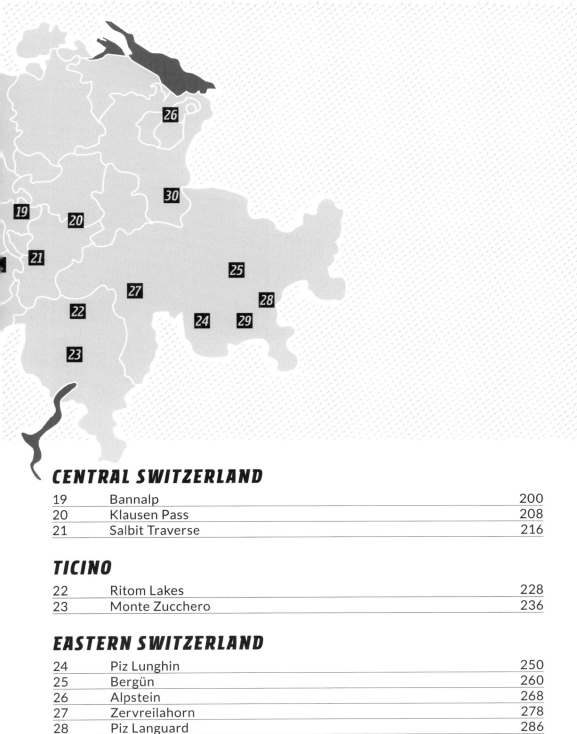

CENTRAL SWITZERLAND

TICINO

EASTERN SWITZERLAND

INTRODUCTION

The Swiss Alps are one of the world's great mountain playgrounds. Here, you can run beside glaciers, weave your way through the clanging bells of a cow herd, and take a time-out at an alpine hut for wild blueberry torte, fresh from the oven. You will end the day tired, dirty, and grinning, having just seen some of the most impressive mountain landscapes imaginable.

There is a wide range of reasons why the Swiss Alps have some of the world's best trail running, but three rise to the top. First, of course, is the sheer majesty of the region. There are 48 peaks over 4,000m in the Swiss Alps. With more than 140 glaciers covering 3,000km^2, it's also one of the most glaciated regions in the world. Scattered below the ice and snow of those high regions are some of the most scenic pastures, forests and farms anywhere.

Second, is the diversity of the regions. It may be that there is no place on the planet with such a wide range of terrain in such a compact space. In a single outing, you can run through forests, over high alpine cols, alongside glaciers, across pastures, and through remote villages. And as the land changes, so do the languages. Even the dialects vary, often dramatically.

Finally, there is Switzerland's famously-reliable transportation. Whether you are in the Engadine or the Valais, nearly every valley in Switzerland is accessible by an ever-efficient network of trains, buses, boats, and trams.

Today, trail running in the Swiss Alps is growing – and rapidly. Years ago farmers would stop and stare, but now the sight of someone dancing down technical terrain wearing compression gear and a tiny pack is far more common. Even the cows are blasé. The number of trail races has exploded, too, by some estimates tripling in the past decade. Popular races like Sierre-Zinal, Eiger Ultra Trail and Trail Verbier St-Bernard now sell out, often in minutes.

This book comes from our desire to share the beauty and diversity of trail running in the Alps. We hope it will both inspire and point the way. The routes can be easily figured out from their descriptions and a good map, or downloaded from the ALPSinsight website.

We've curated thirty routes – plus a unique bonus run – totaling 800km and 56,000m elevation gain. From more than 65,000km of marked trails in Switzerland, this has been a challenging process. We worked to balance a variety of competing criteria, including range of technical difficulty, geographic spread, and degree of physical challenge. Using those measures and others, we've selected these runs to best represent all that Swiss mountain trails offer. We've focused on the heart of the Alps, passing over worthy runs in the broader Prealp areas. Some runners will disagree with our choices, advocating for their favorites. Some runs are known classics, but not all. We've included hidden gems in remote valleys. And although we've been running here for years, we've certainly missed great routes. We'd love to hear about them – if you're willing to share!

We've included bailouts, easier options, overnight possibilities, and bonuses so you can further tailor the runs to your ability, energy, and training expectations. These routes can be used for race training, fitness, fun runs among friends – even as hikes. Most importantly, they are sure to lead you into a landscape where you can make your own adventure.

Our work is done. Now comes the fun part. See which trails inspire you, check your map, and download the tracks. Pack your vest, lace your shoes, and run.

Doug, Kim, Janine, Dan

P.S. We'd love to see your run: #RunTheAlpsSwitzerland

ABOUT THE AUTHORS

DOUG MAYER

has been climbing and trail running in mountain ranges around the world for three decades. In 2013, he founded the tour company Run the Alps. A Contributing Editor for Trail Runner Magazine, he has worked as a Producer for National Public Radio's *Car Talk*. During the making of this book, he made frequent stops for blueberry tortes and friendly hut dogs. He lives in Chamonix, France.

KIM STROM

is a writer and mountain runner always excited to see what's around the next corner or over the next summit. She has experience running and competing in the Alps and throughout Europe, including the first Pierra Menta Été and racing the 2016 and 2017 World Skyrunner Extreme Series. Mostly, she has a contagious passion for the mountains and loves to help motivate and encourage others in their adventures. She is also a Run the Alps ambassador and partner at ALPSinsight.

JANINE & DAN PATITUCCI

are professional mountain sport photographers. Based in the Swiss Alps, Dan & Janine have 20 years of experience shooting mountain sports for the outdoor industry's largest commercial and editorial brands. Their work has taken them to mountains all around the world, from Patagonia to the Himalaya, where they joined their longtime close friend Ueli Steck for numerous climbing expeditions. In 2015, they won a Best American Photography Award for a story shot inside North Korea. To view their work and follow their travels, visit *www.patitucciphoto.com*. In 2016, they created ALPSinsight, a site dedicated to communicating the Alps' mountain sport lifestyle through inspiring experiences, photography, stories and tips.

GETTING READY TO RUN

Run the Alps Switzerland is meant to both inform and inspire. We hope you'll thumb through these pages and want you to grab your shoes for your next big run in the mountains. It's not intended to be a definitive resource, however. We offer these ideas to help get you to the trail and back safely – with tired legs and a huge grin. This book is a starting point. You'll need additional information and an accurate map of the region.

RESEARCH YOUR RUN

Download the Data

Run the Alps Switzerland isn't a guide book that you can hold in your hand through every turn, or that will point out every risk. Route descriptions are not intended to be definitive, so, you'll need a little more detail to stay on the route. For more info about the routes, including downloadable tracks, visit *www.helvetiq.com* or *www.alpsinsight.com*.

Map It

The simplified introductory maps indicate parking, public transport, cable-cars/chair-lifts, huts, various points of interest, and recommended bail-outs. Most runs have a wide array of optional side trails or mountain transportation for lengthening or shortening the day, in case of uncooperative weather, fatigue, or injury. We have mentioned only a few, such as cable-cars, or an easy gravel track to a Postbus stop.

Additional Resources

Here are a few of our preferred resources:

WEATHER	
MeteoSwiss	*www.meteoswiss.admin.ch*

MAPPING	
SwitzerlandMobility	*www.map.schweizmobil.ch*
Swisstopo	*www.swisstopo.admin.ch*

SWISS TRAIL RUNNING INFORMATION AND NEWS	
ALPSinsight	*www.alpsinsight.com*
Run the Alps Blog	*www.runthealps.com/blog*
Swiss Ultra Trail	*www.ultra-trail.ch*
Swiss Trail Racing	*www.runthealps.com/races*

ON THE TRAIL

WHAT TO BRING: TRAIL RUNNING GEAR LIST

Striking the right balance between going light and being safe is a constant work in progress. Here are suggestions for what to bring along based on our experience trail running in the Alps.

GEAR
Phone, programmed with Swiss emergency number 112
Trail shoes
Pack
Weather appropriate clothing
Rain/wind shell
Water/filter
Snack
Cash
Gloves
Buff/hat
Sunscreen
Headlamp
REGA air ambulance insurance card (1414)

OVERNIGHT EXTRAS
Sleeping bag liner
Toiletries- toothbrush/paste
Change of clothes or not
Puffy jacket
Battery

DON'T FORGET COMMON SENSE

The Alps are a true 'Big Mountain' range. There's no shortage of objective hazards like exposure, remoteness, weather, and rockfall with which to contend. Conditions up high and on north facing trails can be very different from the valley. Before heading out, you need to know your abilities and limits in an alpine setting. You need to be physically and mentally prepared for long days in remote mountain settings with changeable weather. If you are unsure, start with an easier run, or team up with a more experienced partner.

TRAIL ETIQUETTE

Trail running is relatively new to many regions, including much of the Alps. As with trail use around the world, there are practical guidelines that are important for mountain runners to follow. These include:

SHARE THE TRAIL
Many of these routes take you to remote valleys and quiet corners, but in a country whose pastime is hiking, you'll likely encounter others on many of Switzerland's trails. Call out a greeting, allow plenty of space, and slow down as necessary if you're approaching someone. No one has priority over other users on the trail.

BEWARE OF DOGS...
From May to October, some shepherds use trained 'Livestock Guardian' dogs to guard their sheep from the occasional marauding wolf, bear, or lynx. Watch for the posted warning signs indicating a working dog, and slow down and walk as you enter their space. For useful tips and a map showing the locations where livestock guardian dogs are working, see *www.protectiondestroupeaux.ch*

...AND BEWARE OF COWS, TOO!
Mother cows are fiercely protective, and will attack if you come too close to their offspring. Watch for the posted signs and take them seriously, detouring around the pasture if you perceive a protective mom!

CLOSING GATES
Many mountain trails pass through land also used for livestock grazing. Please remember to close gates behind you.

RIVER CONTROLS
In the Swiss Alps, hundreds of rivers are actively being managed to avoid the flooding of valleys. These waterways are signposted, and levels may change rapidly and without notice. Move quickly when crossing these rivers.

CASH, PLEASE
Although it's changing, many mountain huts still take cash only. Even if you're not planning to pass by a hut, we recommend bringing CHF along - plans change, and you might find yourself taking an alternate route and glad for a hot mug of Ovomaltine during a rainstorm!

A FEW MORE TIPS

The Swiss Alps are a unique region for running. Over many years, we've developed a few tips that might be useful. These include:

TRANSPORT
Switzerland has an incredible network of trains, buses, and lifts even reaching small side valleys. Check the timetables. Schedules may change based on season and day of the week, and there may be infrequent access to remote areas.

WATER
There are often opportunities to fill up your flasks en route at huts and fountains, but it's a good idea to carry a sufficient amount and be prepared for extra time on the trails. Some runs don't have much support along the way, and it can be useful to carry a small filter for streams.

HUT
Mountain huts in the Alps range from basic shelter with no running water to modern and comfortable structures with full facilities. You can choose to stay over with full board, or stop for fresh baked snacks, drinks, or a full meal during an outing. Be sure to check seasonal closing dates - most huts have wardens during the trail season, from July through mid-September or October. Be sure to leave your muddy shoes outside. Carry cash, make reservations for overnight stays ahead of time, and always follow the posted rules of etiquette.

SNOW
Before you go, consider the aspect and elevation of your run. Slopes over 2,000 meters that are north-facing can hold snow late into the summer. When in doubt, consider bringing along poles and traction such microspikes.

POLES
Consider bringing lightweight running poles for long climbs, and to provide an extra point or two of stability when you're in exposed or slippery spots.

USING THE BOOK

TRAIL MARKERS

The runs in this book follow designated hiking trails. In Switzerland, these trails are marked with signposts, paint, or cairns.

YELLOW ROUTES
Solid yellow signposts indicate trails that are easy to hike.

WHITE-RED-WHITE
Yellow signs with a white-red-white point signify mountain hiking trails. The stripes may also be posted or painted as arrows on rocks. The difficulty, steepness, and exposure of these trails varies. Exposed or technical sections are secured by cables or ladders.

WHITE-BLUE-WHITE
Blue signs and white-blue-white lines signify difficult alpine routes. These routes are to be used by experienced alpine hikers with appropriate equipment. Running these trails requires high fitness, technical skill and caution.

CHOOSE YOUR CHALLENGE

We've rated each trail run on a scale from 1 to 5, with five being the most challenging. Challenge includes a variety of factors: distance, verticality, technicality, remoteness, exposure, and support available en route. The ratings represent opinions only. They are subjective and relative, measured against other runs included in this book. Use them as one of many factors when picking which run is right for you.

1. VALLEY TRAIL
Well-defined paths that don't leave the valley. We have not included any valley trail runs in this guide.

2. MOUNTAIN TRAIL
These runs follow yellow signposted routes or red and white painted markers. They are typically shorter, with less vertical gain, and footing is smoother, but still mountain trails. There are typically huts, fountains and infrastructure along the way. Tour examples: Alpstein, Gantrisch, Bergün.

3.CHALLENGING MOUNTAIN TRAIL

The majority of the runs fall into this category. They stick to yellow signposted routes or red and white painted markers that are generally easy to follow. They usually have long sections of smooth running, but can have some technical footing, and occasionally pass into easier alpine areas. Tour examples: Arolla, Pizol, Sigriswilgrat.

4.ALPINE TRAIL

These trails pass into blue and white marked routes or need to be navigated by cairns. Sure-footedness is required for these more technical trails. May have exposed sections, danger of falling, loose scree, cables or ladders, and you may need to use your hands for balance or light scrambling. These runs generally have big elevation gain and reach more remote areas. Tour examples: Barrhorn, Lac de Louvie, Salbit Traverse.

5.IBEX ONLY

These trails include blue and white marked routes or need to be navigated by cairns. The trail is more technical and exposed sections present the danger of falling. The route may cross loose scree, steep slopes or glacier, and may require the use of cables or ladders and scrambling. These runs can be long, have big elevation gain, and take you to wilder, remote areas without easy bailout. Sudden change in the weather can make the route difficult. Good judgement and alpine experience required. Tour examples: Hardergrat, Lac de Moiry, Monte Zucchero.

WHAT'S YOUR STYLE?

Some trails are smooth dirt that flow serenely through the mountains, others are technical challenges that wander into exposed alpine terrain. We've characterized the following four types of trail styles for each run:

FLOW
Non-technical running on a smooth trail surface, often with gentle curves. You can look up and take in the view without risk of stumbling off the side of the mountain.

TECHNICAL
Requires careful footwork, your full attention, and sometimes your hands!

GRITTY
Gritty trail sections are tough work. You're earning your kilometers on these sections of trail, which often include boulder hopping, scrambling, and digging deep to get through it.

EXPOSED
No falling allowed. Slow down and hold on to chains or cables, because the consequences of a fall are likely to be severe.

EXTRAS

Bonus Summits and Sections
We often recommend shortcuts and bailouts, and on many runs, we've included some of our favorite side trails and detours as a Bonus. Got extra energy for that nearby summit or spectacular viewpoint? We recommend these if you have time and your legs aren't screaming, yet...

Errors, Omissions, and Updates
Spot something in *Run the Alps Switzerland* that needs updating? Help out readers of future editions by letting us know: *runthealps@helvetiq.ch*

Add-Ons
Want the latest news about the book and other offerings? You can stay up to date on route changes and explore more trails by visiting Elevation: ALPSinsight's Trail and Peak Running Resource at *www.alpsinsight.com*

RANKING BY DIFFICULTY

EASY
Bettmeralp
Gental
Piz Lunghin
Bergün
Klausen Pass
Gantrisch
Alpstein
Zervreilahorn
Zinal
Ritom Lakes

MEDIUM
Lauterbrunnen - Grindelwald
Piz Languard
Arolla
Simplon
Stechelberg Obersteinberg Classic
Bannalp
Rosegtal
Sigriswilgrat
Jazzilücke Loop
Zermatt 2-Day Loop
Pizol 5 Lakes Tour
Schynige Platte - Grindelwald
Lac de Louvie

DIFFICULT
Dents Blanches
Barrhorn
Salbit Traverse
Lac de Moiry - Pigne de la Lé
Monte Zucchero
Dent de Morcles
Stechelberg - Kandersteg
Hardergrat

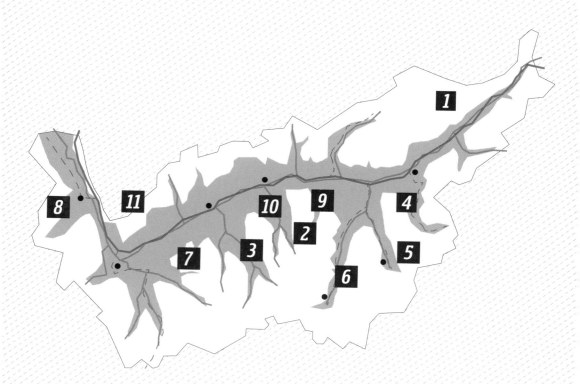

THE RUNS: VALAIS

A third of *Run the Alps Switzerland's* routes are located in the Valais region. In southwest Switzerland, on the border with France and Italy, the Valais is home to the highest peaks in the Swiss Alps. There are 27 summits over 4,000m in height, including the iconic Matterhorn and Switzerland's highest peak, the Dufourspitze, at 4,634m. The canton's French and German-speaking population of 340,000 is focused around the Rhône Valley cities of Sierre, Sion, Martigny and Monthey.

Some of the best mountain running in the region is found in the Pennine Alps, in and above the high valleys that start at the Rhone River. You'll meet Valais black-nosed sheep, the Val d'Hérens cattle, and plenty of Valais farmers - who just might put down their hay rake and give you a "thumbs up" as you run past.

The Valais is a sports-loving region. The Valais Mountain Cup series includes more than three dozen trail races. The canton hosts the famed Sierre-Zinal, Trail Verbier St-Bernard and other internationally-noted races including Matterhorn Ultraks, Les KM de Chando and the Vertical Kilometer of Fully.

BETTMERALP
ALONGSIDE THE ALETSCH GLACIER

MAP

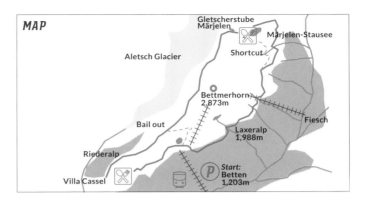

Gletscherstube
Märjelen
Märjelen-Stausee
Aletsch Glacier
Shortcut
Bettmerhorn
2,873m
Fiesch
Bail out
Laxeralp
1,988m
Riederalp
Start:
Betten
1,203m
Villa Cassel

PROFILE

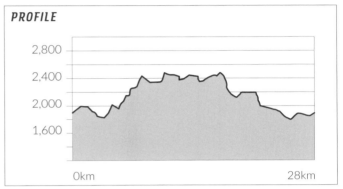

2,800
2,400
2,000
1,600

0km   28km

DIFFICULTY

DISTANCE	28km
ASCENT	1,062m
HIGHEST POINT	2,393m

PEAK SPOTTING
- Aletschhorn
- Matterhorn
- Mönch
- Weisshorn
- Dom
- Weissmies

STYLE
Flow 100%

RUNNING
75 – 100%

COURSE
Loop, clockwise

CANTON
Valais

ACCESS
- Parking: Betten BAB
- Train: Betten
- Lift / Tram: Betten up to
  Bettmeralp (Bettmerhorn)

OTHER CHARACTERISTICS
- Cables / Ladders: No
- Social media hero: Yes

LET'S RUN!

Getting Started
In 2001, the Aletsch glacier, along with the Jungfrau-Aletsch Protected Area, was declared a Unesco World Heritage Site. Nearly 23km long, the Aletsch is the largest glacier in the Alps – but it's rapidly receding. The Pro Natura Center Aletsch reports that the Great Aletsch Glacier is retreating by up to 50m in length each year, as well as shrinking along the edges.

Car-Free
The car-free village of Bettmeralp can only be reached by cable car or a stiff hike up. Tighten your quick-draw laces during the ride up and start racing right out of the tram. Explode from the flock of plaid and khaki-wearing hikers in a blur of brightly colored spandex. *Allez!* Angle towards the Bettmersee and gain height above the town and farms. You're aiming towards Villa Cassel, the nature conservation center, and signposts to Riederfurka. You'll climb here, but it's runnable as you dodge tourists to get to the quieter, wilder backside.

Into the Woods
At Riederfurka, the trail splits just past the info board. Follow the Moränenweg (Ober Aletschweg) which is the middle of three trails, through the nature preserve, a beautiful forest traverse. Angle up following signs toward Moosfluh.

Cool Running
Settle in for a playful and flowing 6km trail high above the glacier. This side of the run follows the curve of the ice, offering big views and a cool breeze from the enormous Aletsch Glacier. You'll round the corner, passing the Märjelensee, then have a chance for food and water at the cozy Gletscherstube, with views across the Märjelen-Stausee.

Smooth Sailing

From Gletscherstube, you cruise on a dirt track around the ridge. High above the towns of Fiesch and Bellwald, stride along the smooth single-track built into the mountainside, and wider pasture roads. An occasional section of ski piste breaks up the route – keep a close eye out for turns as you wend your way around towards the Bettmeralp side of the range.

Back to Bettmeralp

A sloping descent and soft forest trails move you at a quick pace for nearly 10km back to Bettmeralp, where the trams run every half hour back down to Betten.

Why We Love It
Flowing trail alongside Europe's largest and most impressive glacier.

Pro Tip 1
Want to race? Consider this run! Much of the route follows the course of the Aletsch Half Marathon, a race that has been happening for nearly twenty years.

Pro Tip 2
No, you're not reading the signs in Bettmeralp incorrectly. There really is a local recipe called *'cholera'*... it's a delicious leek and potato cake from the Valais.

Pro Tip 3
Running the 1,000m-long tunnel from Gletscherstube quickens the return. It's cool, damp, and sparsely lit. You miss some views, but it's a good shortcut to the ski slope if you linger too long by the Märjelensee.

Bonus
Before or after a break at Villa Cassel, run the flowy 4km-long interpretive loop around the Riederhorn, with signboards about the golden age of Valais tourism a century ago.

Old Growth
On the way to the glacier, you'll pass through the forest. The ancient pines of the Aletsch Forest are at least 600 to 700 years old. They are Switzerland's oldest trees.

Not-to-be-Missed
Don't worry, there's no way you can miss the Aletsch Glacier... but go soon, because like so many of the world's glaciers, it's receding at an alarming rate.

Chill
Make sure you bring a wind shell. Even on warm days, the air coming off millions of tons of ice from the Aletsch Glacier can make part of this run chilly!

MAP

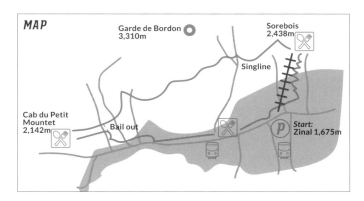

Garde de Bordon ◯
3,310m

Sorebois
2,438m

Singline

Cab du Petit
Mountet
2,142m

Bail out

Start:
Zinal 1,675m

PROFILE

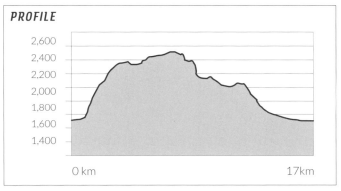

2,600	
2,400	
2,200	
2,000	
1,800	
1,600	
1,400	

0 km   17 km

DIFFICULTY

DISTANCE   17km
ASCENT   1,058m
HIGHEST POINT   2,583m

PEAK SPOTTING
• Dent Blanche
• Zinalrothorn
• Weisshorn
• Bishorn

STYLE
Flow 70%, Technical 30%

RUNNING
75%

CANTON
Valais

COURSE
Loop, counterclockwise

OTHER CHARACTERISTICS
• Cables / Ladders: No
• Social media hero: Yes

ACCESS
• Bus: Zinal Post
• Lift / Tram: The Zinal
  Télépherique up to
  Sorebois

LET'S RUN!

Getting Started
Val d'Anniviers, containing the villages of Chandolin, St. Luc, Grimentz and Zinal, is one of the best trail running regions in the French-speaking Valais. Thanks to the remarkable views along much of the course, the valley's over 40-year-old Sierre-Zinal is often described as the Race of the five 4,000m peaks. The recent addition of the Chando Vertical Race (both single and double vetical kilometer routes) has proven to be a popular.

Going Up
From the town of Zinal, cross the river and follow signs towards the Sorebois lift station. Starting with a steep climb on switchbacks padded with pine needles, it doesn't take long before forest opens to pasture. Head down and hands on your knees, with just a little more effort, you reach Sorebois.

Alpine Route
Don't miss the early turn-off from the ski slope to the start of the single-track. Follow the alpine route, blue and white markers lead toward Petit Mountet. A long ribbon of trail unfolds above the valley, speckled with wildflowers, grazing sheep and cows, plus a few technical steps crossing gushing falls. A narrow rockslide crosses the route. Move cautiously through the big, loose scree.

Descent
Deeply worn gullies lead down to Petit Mountet, overlooking the Glacier de Zinal. From the hut, climb another 70m to traverse through Alpenrosen, and descend swiftly over easy pine forest trail. Meet the road and run less than a kilometer, watching for the right-hand turn to cross two wooden bridges. The final three kilometers flow speedily with the river, flat, back to Zinal.

Why We Love It
Classic Swiss running: high elevation cruising, a quaint mountain hut, and big views of 4,000m summits.

Big Shoes to Fill
In Zinal, next to the tourist office, step into the footprint impressions of Sierre-Zinal winners along the sidewalk.

Pro Tip
Look closely and you'll see the Sierre-Zinal course contouring across pastures on the opposite side of the valley. Stay another day, take the Postbus to St Luc and the funicular to Tignousa to run the best part of 'S-Z' back to town. If you do cross to the other side, be sure to stop into Hotel Weisshorn for their blueberry tart.

Not-to-be-Missed
Valais Blacknose Sheep are raised in the region for wool and meat, and are ridiculously cute. Cross your fingers that some will meander onto your path, as they graze the green slopes of Singline during your traverse.

3 AROLLA
CHASING COLORS IN THE VAL D'HÉRENS

MAP

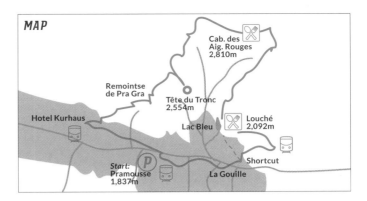

Cab. des
Aig. Rouges
2,810m

Remointse
de Pra Gra

Tête du Tronc
2,554m

Hotel Kurhaus

Lac Bleu

Louché
2,092m

Start:
Pramousse
1,837m

La Gouille

Shortcut

PROFILE

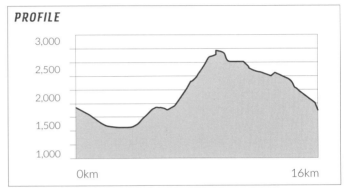

3,000	
2,500	
2,000	
1,500	
1,000	

0km   16km

DIFFICULTY

DISTANCE 16km
ASCENT 1,201m
HIGHEST POINT 2,835m

PEAK SPOTTING
- Mont Collon
- Weisshorn
- Dent Blanche
- Pigne d' Arolla
- Aiguille de la Tsa
- Mont Blanc de Cheilon

STYLE
Flow 80%, Technical 20%

RUNNING
75%

COURSE
Loop, counterclockwise

CANTON
Valais

ACCESS
- Parking: Pramousse
- Bus: Pramousse

OTHER CHARACTERISTICS
- Cables / Ladders: No
- Social media hero: No

LET'S RUN!

Getting Started

In the alluring Val d'Hérens, start from Pramousse (1,850m), with a flat warm-up jog along the river bank folowing signs toward La Gouille. Cross the bridge and follow the stony shoreline before crossing back and heading up through old wooden chalets with traditional carved devils hanging beside the doors, keeping the evil spirits away. Choose signs toward L'Étoile rather than a direct line to Lac Bleu. You'll get to Lac Bleu on a less-used trail with a lower angle for a more runnable climb. Making wider curves through the larch forest, you get to spend more time dreaming about living in one of the cha-lets that overlook the valley.

Colorful Climb

After reaching the treeline and a split in the trail, follow signs to Louché. Just above the old farms, you will reach the aptly named Lac Bleu. From Lac Bleu, the climb be-comes steeper, first through grassy pastures and flowers then changing to more open rocky terrain near L'Étoile. Red rocks and green slopes lead back to a grey moon-scape. A steep, scuffed trail through the rock winds up to the Cabane des Aiguilles Rouges.

Tipping Point

From the hut, it's all downhill following signs to Arolla. A slight drop leads into a sweeping traverse. Gravelly trail strings together S curves for a speedy descent. Admire the milky streams below and pointed peaks across the valley as you begin your descent.

Pra Gra

Stop by Pra Gra, a cluster of abandoned wooden farms. The trail drops through pastures, grazing black cows, and a short descent through the forest to finish. On the last few hundred meters descent, follow the trail crossing the dirt road to cut through its longer switchbacks. Don't miss the turn-off just before Hotel Kurhaus. Head down through the pasture, and speed through the larch forest sloping back to Pramousse. If you do miss the turn and reach the hotel, stop for a drink at the bar before finish-ing the last 2km through the larch.

Why We Love It

The narrow Val d'Hérens is quiet and wild, sitting beneath glaciers and jagged summits. From Lac Bleu to Aiguilles Rouges, the climb is a bit of a grind, but leads you into a moonscape. Once you're at the top, it's easy footing and great running.

Not-to-be-Missed

On the way down, don't miss the 10 minute out-and-back detour to Tête du Tronc (2,549m) where you can see your entire loop leading up to the perched hut and wrapping along the basin traverse.

Pro Tip

Stick around to explore the 200km of marked running routes in the Evolène Region.

Carnaval

Come back to the Val d'Hérens in the winter for the Carnaval d'Evolène. Joining in the week-long Epiphany rituals might help protect the towns from avalanches, allow spring to arrive – and welcome a new trail running season, too!

SIMPLON

A PATH AWAY FROM THE PASS

MAP

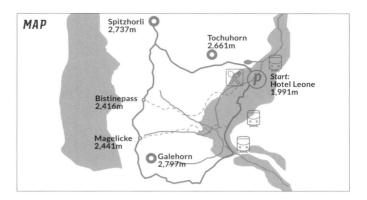

Spitzhorli 2,737m
Tochuhorn 2,661m
Start: Hotel Leone 1,991m
Bistinepass 2,416m
Magelicke 2,441m
Galehorn 2,797m

PROFILE

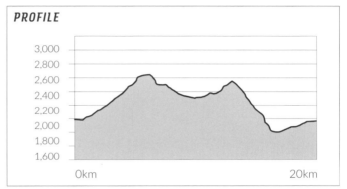

3,000
2,800
2,600
2,400
2,200
2,000
1,800
1,600

0km   20km

DIFFICULTY

DISTANCE	20km
ASCENT	1,211m
HIGHEST POINT	2,737m

PEAK SPOTTING
- Bietschhorn
- Fletschhorn
- Weissmies
- Monte Leone
- Lagginhorn
- Mischabel group

PEAK TAGGING
- Spitzhorli 2,737m

CANTON
Valais

OTHER CHARACTERISTICS
- Cables / Ladders: No
- Social media hero: No

STYLE
Flow 80%, Technical 20%

RUNNING
75%

COURSE
Loop, counterclockwise

ACCESS
- Parking: Hotel Monte Leone
- Bus: Simplon, Monte Leone

LET'S RUN!

Getting Started
Turn your back on the busy pass, face the mountains, and head into the wild for a few free-flowing hours of trail running. Thanks to the high elevation of the pass road, today's run avoids the forested, uphill start of so many runs in the Alps. Follow signs for the Gondo Marathon course past a tiny cluster of houses at Hopsche, and continue to Üsseri Nanzlicke. At this point, you've already climbed 800m – the bulk of this route's gain!

Summit Sideline
From the intersection at Üsseri Nanzlicke, take the quick out-and-back to reach the rocky heights of the Spitzhorli (2,737m). This addition adds a little more than 100m of vertical gain, and the view is well worth it.

Flow Time
Flying over kilometers 6-12 on the traverse, don't forget to take a moment to look over your shoulder at the triangular Bietschhorn. Next, you'll race over a flowing, single-track traverse that wraps along the hillside. After Straffolsee, join the national #6 hiking route, Alpenpässe-Weg. Wilder terrain, glowing green slopes, and waterfalls pull you deeper into the valley as you arc through the furthest curve of the loop. Mostly angling down with short uphill rolls, be careful not to miss the split to pop up to Sirwoltesattel (2,620 m), a brief climb, 11.5km from the start.

Bombing Down
At the saddle, you'll reach the military training area and start a rapid, technical descent beside rushing waterfalls. Black and white goats startle from their grazing as you drop toward a small cluster of lakes. After crossing a river, there's only a bit more technical downhill towards Engiloch. You can now see Alter Spittel, the Old Hospice, in the distance. There's not far to go!

Smooth Moving
Make a quick stop by the stone houses at Chlusmatte to fill your flasks at the water trough. From here, you'll follow brown signs for the Stockalperweg, a gentle trail along the Chrummbach, to Nideralp. The rolling dirt trail eases your re-entry into civilization, leading past the old hospice, cheese farms, stone cottages, and finally back to Simplon Pass.

Why We Love It
This run has a wild feeling, free of mountain infrastructure, with a little bit of everything: runnable climbs, kilometers of flowing single-track, a rocky downhill, and a finish that's a good shakeout for the legs.

Not-to-be-Missed
A dip in one of the several lakes en route, or a quick clean-up at the lake by the parking area.

Run Gondo
Check out the Gondo Marathon, a unique double-marathon over two days, which runs through the pass. The race is held in memory of the border hamlet of the same name, which was destroyed by a landslide in October, 2000.

Pro Tip
Take a few minutes to enjoy the hospice across the road. Built by Napoleon in 1801, the hospice and monastery is open year-round and accommodates 130 guests. It's run by the same Augustinian Catholic monks who operate its more famous sister at St. Bernard Pass.

Sordid Past

Simplon Pass was one of the first routes through the Alps and has been traveled by mercenaries and smugglers since the Stone Age. Napoleon built the first road here, and the Swiss military built tunnels throughout the pass, installing guns in the narrow walls of Gondo Canyon to defend the road against the Italian Fascists during WWII. Today, the only tunnels in use are the 20km-long ones that trains use between Brig, Switzerland and Iselle di Trasquera, Italy.

Incoming!

Here's a sign that you don't see too often on a trail run. Several times during the year, the Swiss military trains in the Simplon Pass area. Double check the training schedule at *www.simplon.ch* before you go, to make sure you won't have to shout 'Incoming!' during your run.

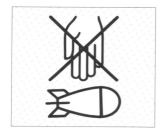

5 JAZZILÜCKE LOOP
INTO ITALY FROM SAAS ALMAGELL

MAP

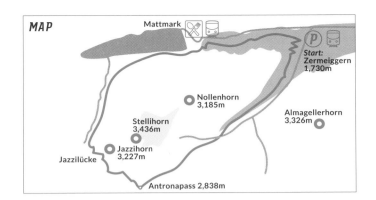

PROFILE

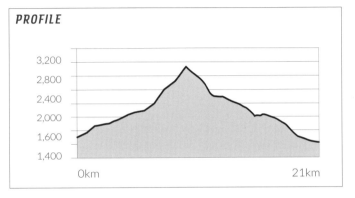

3,200
2,800
2,400
2,000
1,600
1,400

0km   21km

DIFFICULTY

DISTANCE	21km
ASCENT	1,360m
HIGHEST POINT	3,083m

PEAK SPOTTING
• Monte Rosa
• Dom
• Mischabel Group
• Weissmies

STYLE
Flow 60%, Technical 30%, Exposure 10%

CANTON
Valais

RUNNING
75%

COURSE
Loop, clockwise

OTHER CHARACTERISTICS
• Cables / Ladders: Yes
• Social media hero: No

ACCESS
• Parking: Zer Meiggeru
• Bus: Zermeiggern

LET'S RUN!

Getting Started
This route leads over an ancient salt and smuggling route, exploring a less traveled corner of the Swiss Alps that peeks over the border to Italy. Getting started just outside quiet Saas Almagell, runnable switchbacks carry you the first few hundred meters gain through soft larch forest. Signs direct you to Almageller Furgg.

Furggtälli
Popping out of the forest soon after your start, the river leads you deep into the Furggtälli valley. The trail is a long, low incline ramp that grows wilder, more secluded, and leads to rockier more technical running the higher and further you travel.

Benvenuto in Italia
At the Antronapass, signposts switch to Italian and you cross the border to skirt around the Jazzihorn before returning to Switzerland at the next pass, Jazzilücke.

Into the Ofental
From the dramatic ridges, descend to the Ofental. You might not see another person in this valley as you circle the Mittelgrat. The remote trail provides a blend of technical and fast running. Here, you can fly, but stay focused on what's underfoot. The initially steep descent levels off, and the trail looks like you might run off the edge of the world.

Dam!
Reaching the edge, the next section of trail drops you down to the Stausee Mattmark, a sudden return to civilization. Stride out alongside the turquoise water of the dam, a fast flat section shared with the crowds.

Fast Finish
Tuck into the forest at the end of the dam for a rapid descent to Zermeiggern. Springy trail cuts across the wide switchbacks of the main road and returns you to the start.

Why We Love It
This trail has a little bit of everything: soft runnable climb, exposure, technical rock hopping, and a speedy downhill. Rockier footing, and some technical sections near the Italian border make this a more challenging run.

Not-to-be-Missed
Your own movement. This is a run that's as much about the beauty of running as it is the landscape.

Pro Tip
Watch your step. Don't trip on the rocky trail. There's so much to look at you'll need to stop once in a while to take it all in.

Go Wild
There's no infrastructure in these wild valleys, so carry what you need.

Bonus
Scramble up an extra 150m to the Jazzihorn to tag a peak.

Fighting Cows
In the Valais, keep an eye out for cows with numbers painted on them. The Hérens cows compete to establish their hierarchy in the herd.

Lost for Words
This trail is so good, your running buddies might spend more time grunting their satisfaction than finding words to describe it. Oh! Woah! Yaaaaaa! EEEEE!

ZERMATT 2-DAY LOOP
BENEATH THE MATTERHORN

DAY 1

MAP

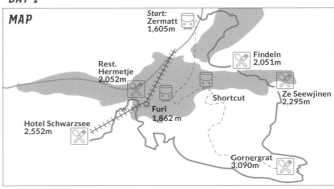

Start:
Zermatt
1,605m

Findeln
2,051m

Rest.
Hermetje
2,052m

Ze Seewjinen
2,295m

Shortcut

Furi
1,862 m

Hotel Schwarzsee
2,552m

Gornergrat
3,090m

PROFILE

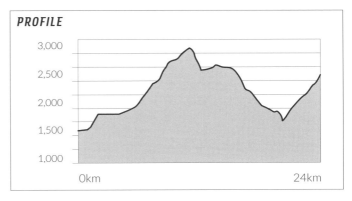

3,000
2,500
2,000
1,500
1,000

0km   24km

DIFFICULTY

DISTANCE   24km
ASCENT   2,304m
HIGHEST POINT   3,094m

PEAK SPOTTING
• Matterhorn
• Weisshorn
• Mettelhorn
• Monte Rosa
• Liskamm
• Castor and Pollux
• Breithorn
• Täschhorn
• Alphubel

STYLE
Flow 90%, Technical 10%

RUNNING
75%

COURSE
Loop as Multi-Day, clockwise

CANTON
Valais

ACCESS
• Parking: Täsch
• Train: Zermatt
• Tram: Gornergrat, Furi,
  Schwarzsee

OTHER CHARACTERISTICS
• Cables / Ladders: No
• Social media hero: Yes

DAY 1

Getting Started

From the ever-busy Zermatt train station, head downhill, and pick up the signs for Ried as you twist and turn your way up from the valley. Switchbacks climb along the route of three of the Matterhorn Ultraks races onto nearly flat single-track. You can zoom along, occasionally glancing up at the Matterhorn or down to town. A cluster of chalets at Findeln offer a chance to refuel, before dropping briefly to cross the Findelbach.

Up a Kilometer

It's time to go up! Bearing straight ahead at a switchback, cross an alpine ski trail, then climb through Arolla pines and past a jumble of rock scree. Enjoy the big views across to Trift, as you head past the Ze Seewijnen restaurant, and take a gravel road. From the road crossing above the hotel, it's steady climbing as you switchback above the treeline. The big Zermatt views become humongous. Just under a kilometer past Gornergratsee, swing right, and up an unmarked trail to meet the ridge.

Run on the Wild Side

Without going all the way to Gornergrat, take a left off the ridge onto a blue and white marked trail, a steep drop down to the junction. The most peaceful running of the day flows along this smooth trail, as you climb with the Gornergletscher on your left. Look across the glacier, and you'll spot the Swiss Alpine Club's ultra-modern and efficient Monte Rosa hut. Coast past the crowds at the Riffelsee, veering left around the lake. You'll cruise through high pastures, staying left at junctions as you coast down towards Furi. Polished rock during the final descent asks for more attention from your technical dancing. Cross the Gornera over the dramatic hanging bridge, and rush along ski and hiking trails to Furi.

Ending on a High Note

The day's final climb weaves between the sheep and wooden barns at Furi. Dig down for those last 650m, as you switchback through forests, then pastures, and up the slope to Schwarzsee – where it's time for a shower, dinner, and a chance to kick back and take in one of the best views in all the Valais. Enjoy the rest at the end of Day 1, knowing what comes tomorrow will be even better!

DAY 2

MAP

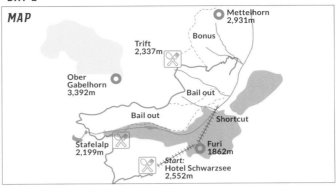

PROFILE

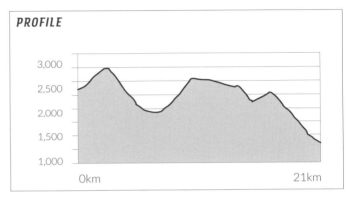

0km   21km

DIFFICULTY

DISTANCE   21km
ASCENT   1,172m
HIGHEST POINT   2,931m

STYLE
Flow 90%, Technical 10%

RUNNING
75%

PEAK SPOTTING
• Matterhorn
• Weisshorn
• Mettelhorn
• Monte Rosa
• Liskamm
• Castor and Pollux
• Breithorn
• Täschhorn
• Alphubel

COURSE
Loop as Multi-Day, clockwise

ACCESS
• Parking: Täsch
• Train: Zermatt
• Tram: Gornergrat, Furi,
  Schwarzsee

CANTON
Valais

OTHER CHARACTERISTICS
• Cables / Ladders: No
• Social media hero: Yes

DAY 2

Wake Up

Fresh in the morning, head out from Hotel Schwarzsee after breakfast and start towards the Matterhorn. No directions needed. A short climb and amazing views draw you towards the mountain. Follow signs toward Hörnlihütte, speeding along the smooth trail high on the Hörnliweg. At the split, don't make the final climb to the busy hut, but instead take a sharp right off the ridge following signs toward Zermatt.

To the Other Side

The descent is steep and smooth, a quick way to lose meters. This is a downhill to savor, fast and fluid. Cross the road and continue down, descending only as far as Stafelalp. From there follow signs toward Trift, over the river, and begin the next climb up to Trift on the other side of the valley.

Traversing to Trift

After the climb, 5km of smooth traverse unravels high above the valley. Massive views pull you along the single-track, and you can take them all in because the trail is pristine, uninterrupted by anything to stumble over. A quick drop winds down to Trift Hut. Stop to refuel with home-made iced tea made with lemon, orange juice and sugar, and an apple torte fresh from the oven. You might want to linger here. It's tempting to stay another night and do the Mettelhorn for sunrise, or push on and add it to the day's route.

Finale

Getting going again, a short climb takes you up from Trift, and then it's all downhill to Zermatt. A sloping traverse leads into wide sweeping switchbacks that tighten as you drop further into the forest. Your descent quickens, as you approach the main station after an outstanding tour.

Why We Love It
Non-stop Matterhorn views and some of the smoothest single-track in the Alps. The loop hits many of the highlights of the area in one big tour above Zermatt, which is never far away.

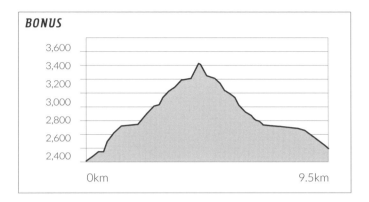

BONUS

Bonus
A high perch all alone above busy Zermatt, the out-and-back to the Mettelhorn (3,406m) adds 9.5km and 1,059m+ with a small glacier crossing. On the second day, a side trip to this mini-Matterhorn is a good test for the legs, more than doubling your final descent to Zermatt. The pointed summit is worth the effort and the quad trashing for its high perspective across the valley and far-from-it-all feeling.

Pro Tip
There are lots of ways to adjust this 2-day tour. Do more with the bonus or less using the trains and lifts to Gornergrat, Furi, or Schwarzsee. Each day can be run as individual loops if limited to one day.

Runner's High
Both days have high altitude cruising... acclimatizing helps.

Quick Climb
In 2015, Swiss climber Dani Arnold successfully climbed the Matterhorn's North Face in a new record time of 1h 46min. Arnold's time knocked ten minutes off the previous record, set by Ueli Steck in 2009.

7 LAC DE LOUVIE
JOURNEY THROUGH THREE COLS

MAP

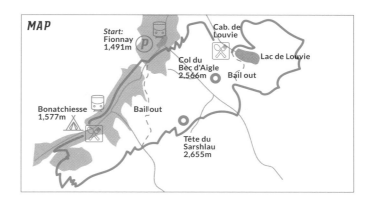

Start:
Fionnay
1,491m

Cab. de
Louvie

Lac de Louvie

Col du
Bec d'Aigle
2,566m

Bail out

Bonatchiesse
1,577m

Bailout

Tête du
Sarshlau
2,655m

PROFILE

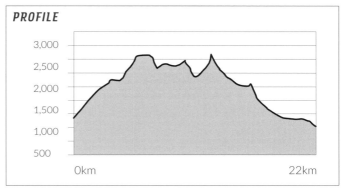

3,000
2,500
2,000
1,500
1,000
500

0km   22km

DIFFICULTY

DISTANCE   22km
ASCENT   1,919m
HIGHEST POINT   2,648m

PEAK SPOTTING
- Grand Combin
- Mont Blanc de Cheillon
- Le Pleureur

STYLE
Flow 60%, Technical 30%,
Exposure 10%

CANTON
Valais

RUNNING
50 – 75%

COURSE
Loop, clockwise

OTHER CHARACTERISTICS
- Cables / Ladders: No
- Social media hero: No

ACCESS
- Parking: Fionnay
- Bus: Fionnay

LET'S RUN!

Getting Started
Start out towards Lac de Louvie from Fionnay, a small village near the back of the Val de Bagnes. The steep 700m climb turns its way through goat pastures and forest before opening to Cabane de Louvie overlooking the lake.

Through Three Cols
Edging along the lake, you continue to climb to Col Termin (2,648m), the high point of the run with massive views across the valley to the Combin range. Coming through the col to steep grassy slopes, you'll descend quickly, following signs toward Col de Louvie. Drop down to the river at Plan de Gole before beginning the climb to the next high pass, Col du Bec d'Aigle (2,567m). From this second pass, it's a traversing down-slope to reach Le Dâ. The traverse and climb to Col du Sarshlau (2,622m) is rocky, leading to a narrow passage between sharp towers. These jagged 6km connecting the cols are a wild journey, but once you step through the third narrow pass, it's all downhill. Over the edge a curving smooth descent awaits.

Tour des Écuries
Traverse grassy trails through sheep pastures, beside stone stables the Écurie du Crêt and Écurie du Vasevay, and toward gushing waterfalls. From the Écurie du Vase-vay, tight snaking turns drop lower and lower while the mountains grow higher above you. Follow signs back to Fionnay along a perfectly angled forest descent, soft and speedy.

River Return
When you reach the valley floor, pass through the camp, past a few small buildings in Bonatschiesse, and follow the flat river path. Roll through a few forested sections and finally drop onto the road.

Fionnay 1h25
Bonatchiesse 1h15
Vasevay 30min
Mauvoisin 1h40
Le Dâ 1h35
Louvie 2h50
Ecurie du Vasevay

Why We Love It

It's not just a run, but a journey. The circuit climbs to a picturesque alpine lake, threads through three cols (Termin, Bec d'Aigle, Col du Sarshlau), and skims along pastures, forest, and riverside.

Not-to-be-Missed

Questions are mounted on ski poles to keep you distracted from the effort of the first climb. How many turns does the trail make on the way up to Cabane de Louvie? If you want to find out, ask the hut keeper for the answer sheet (in French).

Pro Tip

Don't lose momentum on the five-star descent from Écurie du Vasevay. Smooth race-track curves have you speeding down 3km of total bliss.

Trophée des Combins

One of the oldest mountain races in the Alps is held each August on the slopes across the valley. For more than 50 years, runners have toed the line to link Fionnay to Panossière (Length: 7.8km / Gain: 1,180m). Challenge yourself on this uphill course, join the camaraderie, and discover its unique history.

MAP

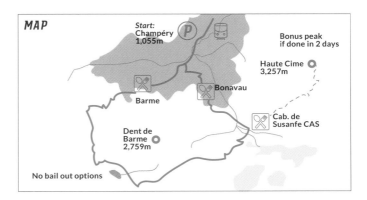

Start:
Champéry
1,055m

Bonus peak
if done in 2 days

Haute Cime
3,257m

Bonavau

Barme

Cab. de
Susanfe CAS

Dent de
Barme
2,759m

No bail out options

PROFILE

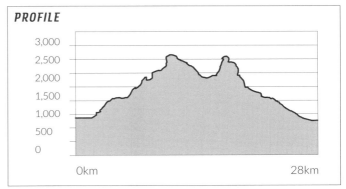

0km   28km

DIFFICULTY

DISTANCE   28km
ASCENT   2,240m
HIGHEST POINT   2,555m

PEAK SPOTTING
• Dents du Midi
• Mont Blanc

STYLE
Flow 40%, Technical 20%,
Gritty 30%, Exposure 10%

CANTON
Valais

RUNNING
50%

OTHER CHARACTERISTICS
• Cables / Ladders: Yes
• Social media hero: No

COURSE
Loop, clockwise

ACCESS
• Parking: Champéry
  Grand Paradis
• Train: Champéry

LET'S RUN!

Getting Started

Leaving charming Champéry and passing the camp-
ground at Grand Paradis, start up a steep forest climb.
The early meters pass quickly following signs through
Bonavau and a grassy traverse toward Susanfe. Before
reaching the Cabane de Susanfe, follow the split leading
to Col des Ottans.

Iron Way

Rocky fields suddenly create a moonscape, with a worn
track snaking higher. You gain elevation as you work your
way toward a vertical rock wall. It looks impassable, but
the corner is fitted with cables and ladders. You emerge
from a narrow chimney and continue upwards to the col.

Frontière

Edging along the Swiss-French border, the broad ridgeline rises to the Tête des Ottans and then down to Col
du Sagerou. A quarter of the run passes over the French
border, continuing with a sloping traverse before dropping to Lac de la Vogealle. (Head down to Refuge de la
Vogealle if you're ready for lunch or just a snack and a
drink.) Keep to the right side of the lake, and from its end,
start the climb up to Pas au Taureau. The way is rocky
leading you to the second high col. From here it's a steep
scree descent to Col de Bossetan and back across the
Swiss border.

Below Dents Blanches

The steep descent over white rock continues. You'll
need your hands and the occasional cables to help you
down as you follow signs toward Barme and Champéry.
The trail intersects a dirt road at Luibronne beside the
Torrent de Barme. After some tricky footing, it's a
relaxing finish through peaceful farms and forests below
the towering Dents Blanches. If you're ready for a break,
several auberges await at Barme. Once you've passed
through Barme, you'll soon recognize Les Clous and your
way back to town.

Why We Love It

For the challenge as well as the beauty. This run has long steep climbs, a technical descent, and hops over the French border for a bit.

Not-to-be-Missed

Watch for ibex camouflaged in the rocks as you're passing through their playground back into Switzerland.

Pro Tip

There are no bailouts to get you easily back to where you started. Plan to dig deep for all those meters up and down.

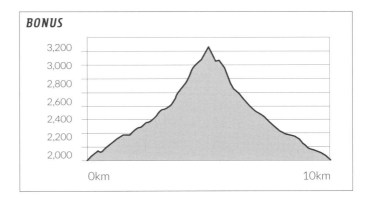

Bonus

Make it a two day run. The stiff climb up to Haute Cime is worth the effort. Add 10km and 1,307m+/- to reach the precipitous summit at 3,257m with a thrilling 360° view. Spend the night at Cabane de Susanfe and finish the loop the following day.

DDM Trail

Make an ultra-long weekend in the area, looping 57km around the Dents du Midi range. Following the course of the DDM Trail, one of the Alps' oldest trail races, you'll see many angles of the Dents du Midi, one of the most frequently painted ranges in the Swiss Alps.

BARRHORN
SWITZERLAND'S HIGHEST TRAIL

MAP

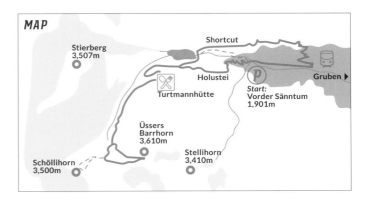

- Stierberg 3,507m
- Shortcut
- Holustei
- Turtmannhütte
- Gruben ▶
- Start: Vorder Sänntum 1,901m
- Üssers Barrhorn 3,610m
- Stellihorn 3,410m
- Schöllihorn 3,500m

PROFILE

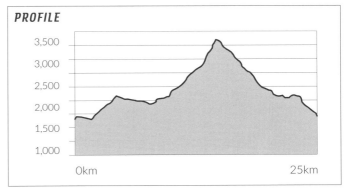

3,500		
3,000		
2,500		
2,000		
1,500		
1,000		

0km   25km

DIFFICULTY

DISTANCE   25km
ASCENT   2,033m
HIGHEST POINT   3,610m

PEAK SPOTTING
- Mischabel and Monte Rosa Ranges
- Weisshorn
- Bishorn
- Dom

PEAK TAGGING
- Üssers Barrhorn 3,610m

CANTON
Valais

OTHER CHARACTERISTICS
- Cables / Ladders: Yes
- Social media hero: Yes

STYLE
Flow 60%, Technical 30%, Gritty 10%

RUNNING
50 – 75%

COURSE
Loop, counterclockwise

ACCESS
- Parking: Vorder Sänntum
- Bus: Gruben

LET'S RUN!

Getting Started

From Vorder Sänntum or Gruben, in the back of the narrow Turtmann Valley, follow a worn path in the grass along the river. The first 500m climb starts from a cluster of farms midway between the two. Follow signs toward Chalte Berg up through soft forest trail to meet the road at Massstafel. An unmarked split just past a fountain angles left to leave the road for a small trail to continue the climb.

Berry-Lined Traverse

A rolling, mostly downhill traverse pulls you through low shrubs and blueberry bushes toward distant, wild peaks, glaciers and rocky moraine before dropping to the Turtmannsee. Cross the dam and take the trail that follows the line of the river. Signs direct to Turtmannhütte (Steinmannliweg) and a rockier trail leads further back into the valley and up to Turtmannhütte.

Getting High

From Turtmannhütte, the trail becomes alpine. You soon reach a short cabled section and the barren moraine. Follow cairns to wind through loose gravel. Watch for a cairn at 3,100m, where the trail splits and follow the trail to the left. A steep push delivers you directly to Üssers Barrhorn, Switzerland's highest peak reachable by trail.

Retrace the Trail

Start the return only as far as 3,500m, then stay high and follow the variant toward the col. A signpost at the col designates the split to Topali via Schöllijoch and Turtmannhütte. Swerve over a rapid descent to meet the trail you came up and retrace the route to the hut.

Finale

At Turtmannhütte, stop for a hearty Rösti or a well-deserved *Schwarzwälder Kirschtorte* (Black Forest cake) before finishing the final 5km. Descend the way you came up, but don't drop to the dam. Stay higher at the wooden lift cart and traverse high to gather more blueberries before dropping to Holustei. The final meters disappear quickly, and you are suddenly back on the valley floor.

Valais - Barrhorn | 101

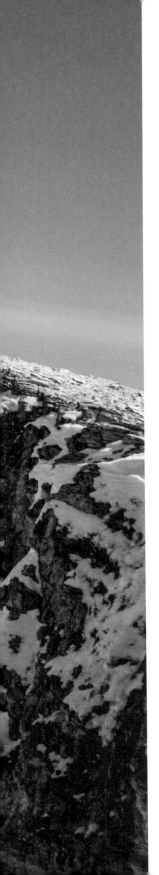

Why We Love It
Starting in a remote, dead-end valley, Switzerland's highest official trail reaches 3,610m, the summit of the Barrhorn.

Not-to-be-Missed
Besides big views of glaciers and peaks above, down by your feet there are mushrooms, blueberries, and edelweiss along the way.

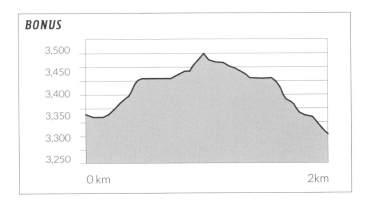

Bonus
Tag the Schöllihorn (3,499m) by adding 2km and a 160m gain. The short loop from the col takes you to a wide bump of a summit with big mountain backdrops.

Pro Tip
At high altitude, the temperature can drop below freezing even on warm summer days. Take cold weather layers including gloves.

Slipping Up
Early morning can be icy on the higher trail sections. Consider a later start to let things thaw.

MAP

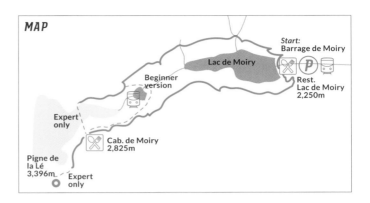

Start:
Barrage de Moiry

Lac de Moiry

Beginner version

Rest.
Lac de Moiry
2,250m

Expert only

Cab. de Moiry
2,825m

Pigne de la Lé
3,396m

Expert only

PROFILE

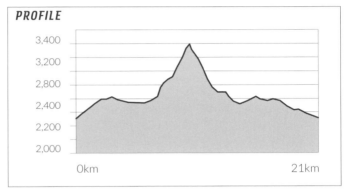

3,400
3,200
2,800
2,400
2,200
2,000

0km   21km

DIFFICULTY

DISTANCE   21km
ASCENT   1,457m
HIGHEST POINT   3,396m

PEAK SPOTTING
• Dent Blanche
• Grand Cornier
• Ober Gabelhorn
• Zinalrothorn
• Besso
• Weisshorn
• Trifthorn

PEAK TAGGING
• Pigne de la Lé 3,396m

CANTON
Valais

OTHER CHARACTERISTICS
• Cables / Ladders: No
• Social media hero: Yes

STYLE
Flow 40%, Technical 40%,
Exposed 20%

RUNNING
75%

COURSE
Loop, counterclockwise

ACCESS
• Parking: Barrage de Moiry
• Bus: Barrage (Moiry VS)

LET'S RUN!

Getting Started
Cross the dam. On the other side, follow signs for Tour du Lac 2500, which circles the lake staying mostly at 2,500m elevation. The rolling traverse leads into pastures higher along the lake.

On the Ice
Leaving the grassy slopes for a rocky moraine, approximately 8km into the run, follow cairns to drop to the glacier. Only cross the glacier when conditions allow, otherwise take the trail passing by Lac de Châteaupré at the earlier junction.

Time to Climb
Stepping off the ice, yellow paint leads up a loose trail to Cabane de Moiry. From the hut, a steep and rocky trail moves you up to Col du Pigne to overlook the Zinal valley. Carefully choose your way up, following the ridge to Pigne de la Lé, a final scramble of 255m, for an amazing overlook of the Glacier de Moiry.

Coming Down
Retreat by the same route back to the hut, then zigzag down to meet grassy elevation. After descending from the hut, the trail splits into three. Keep to the highest trail for the traverse.

Tour Traverse
Again on the Tour du Lac 2500, pass the Fêta d'Août de Châteaupré on the way back to Moiry Barrage. Ride this perfectly smooth trail traverse until you arrive above the dam for a brief downhill finish.

Why We Love It
Fast trails for running with an adventurous side – crossing the Moiry Glacier and a serious scramble.

Not-to-be-Missed
Keep an eye open for edelweiss growing on the grassy traverse leading back to the dam.

Pro Tip
Caution on the glacier crossing: go when the hut is wardened, when winter snow is off the glacier, and carry at least one pole for stability on the sloppy, sloping section leaving the glacier.

Other Side of the Aiguilles
If you've run the Zinal valley, you're looking down on the trails from the other side of the Aiguilles de la Lé.

Off the Ice
You can make this an easier run by omitting the glacier crossing and summit scramble. After 6km of easy trail running, drop to Lac de Châteaupré to cross to the opposite side of the valley and climb to Cabane de Moiry by the main trail. From the hut, the route is the same but turns back at the Col du Pigne. Still a great 20km option if you want to avoid the ice.

11

DENT DE MORCLES
A LONG DAY OVER THE VALAIS

MAP

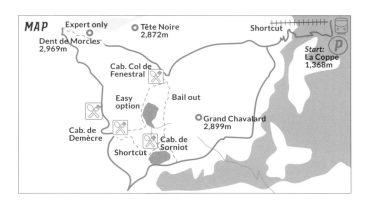

Expert only

Dent de Morcles
2,969m

Tête Noire
2,872m

Shortcut

Start:
La Coppe
1,368m

Cab. Col de
Fenestral

Easy
option

Bail out

Grand Chavalard
2,899m

Cab. de
Demècre

Cab. de
Sorniot

Shortcut

PROFILE

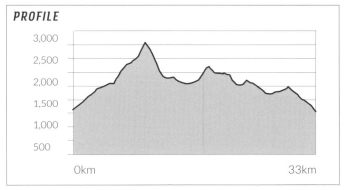

3,000
2,500
2,000
1,500
1,000
500

0km   33km

DIFFICULTY

PEAK SPOTTING
• Dents du Midi
• Mont Blanc
• Grand Combin

PEAK TAGGING
• Dent de Morcles 2,969m

CANTON
Valais / Vaud

OTHER CHARACTERISTICS
• Cables / Ladders: Yes
• Social media hero: No

DISTANCE	33km
ASCENT	2,357m
HIGHEST POINT	2,969m

STYLE
Flow 50%, Technical 30%,
Gritty 10%, Exposed 10%

RUNNING
75%

COURSE
Loop, counterclockwise

ACCESS
• Parking: La Coppe/Centre
  Sportif Cantonal, or at base
  of the lift
• Bus: Ovronnaz, croisée du
  centre
• Lift / Tram: Jorasse

LET'S RUN!

Getting Started

From Ovronnaz, hiking signs lead to Col de Fénestral, starting with a forest trail to a wide dirt road. The climb to the farm at Petite Pré is sometimes steep but often runnable. Reaching the grassy plateau, it's easy running under rocky towers until the switchbacks to Col de Fénestral. As you pop over the col, you'll be struck by a sudden view of the Mont Blanc massif. The full-service Cabane du Fénestral awaits you on the other side.

Expert Track

Heads up! It's necessary to be comfortable on technical terrain to tackle the narrow edge winding down from the summit. Careful with your footing if you choose this track.

From the cabane, the trail becomes a blue and white painted alpine route. An airy traverse flows towards a moonlike landscape and a wild climb that grows steeper the higher you go. A yellow painted Souriez (reminder to smile) splits the route: up to the summit or down to start your descent. After a short scramble to the summit of Dent de Morcles, follow the trail marked with cairns and blue paint to begin the first descent. This technical section is airy and loose, and requires caution.

Back on Solid Ground

Continuing the steep descent toward not-so-distant Lake Geneva, a tight 180 degree turn-around eventually directs you towards Col du Demècre. If you reach Rionda, you've run too far. Here, you begin a rolling, grassy traverse below towering rock walls and turrets. 4kms pass at a quick pace, leading to the next climb. Now up toward Col du Demècre and through Diabley, following signs to Portail de Fully.

Traverse

Hanging in through those tough meters is now rewarded with a 5km traverse of first-rate running! There are great views as you curve around the Portail de Fully and angle toward the Lac de Fully. Staying above the lakes, follow the wide path to L'Erié.

Forest Finish

Pass through the parking lot at L'Erié, down the road to the first switchback, and into the forest towards Ovronnaz. Following signs for Ovronnaz to Petit Pré, you arrive back at the dirt road from the morning's ascent as your tired legs retrace the forest steps that started this run – but this time, you'll have the satisfaction of a big adventure ticked off!

Downsize the Run

The full loop is quite demanding and requires good footing and solid fitness. The good news is, you can easily shorten the run and still get plenty of flowy, less demanding trail running. Follow the easier option from the beautiful new Cabane du Fénestral down to Lac Supérieur de Fully, and then up to a second newly rebuilt cabin at Col du Demècre. Want to take it really easy? Skip the Col du Demècre, and head straight for the lower Lac de Fully, and meet the return trail there. You will miss a great little cabin with views to the Dents du Midi and Lake Geneva, but you'll still enjoy the fun cruise to come.

Why We Love It
Sweeping views across the Valais to the high Alps while cruising along smooth traverses. Some technical sections combined with tons of first-rate running.

Not-to-be-Missed
Old military barracks built into the cliffs on the descent route from Dent de Morcles. It is not permitted to stay overnight because of the risk of landslides.

Get Your Antioxidants
If you're there in early August, watch for wild blueberries to sustain the climb up to Col du Demècre.

Lift Up
Want to save your legs for the long day ahead? The lift to Jorasse saves you 600m. Meet up with the tour at Petit Pré.

Pro Tip
Take poles for the loose descent above the Grande Vire, and a headlamp too – it might be a long day!

PORTRAIT

MARTIN ANTHAMATTEN

Martin Anthamatten is one of Switzerland's top-ranked ski mountaineering racers. Born and raised in Zermatt, he continues to call the resort town at the base of the Matterhorn his home. A certified Swiss Mountain Guide like his two brothers, Martin's primary job is with the Swiss Border Guard. He's also one of the country's best-known trail runners. Ranging across the Alps, from the Engadine to Valais, he spends the summer months looking for new trails and racing the Skyrunning series.

My parents were not athletes, but when we were young, we'd all go into the mountains. Slowly, though, not fast like now! Those trips gave my brothers and me a deep enthusiasm for the mountains. My brothers are involved in mountain sports, too. Sam is a top freeride skier. He competes in the Freeride World Tour. Simon is a strong alpinist who climbs both rock and ice.

As a mountain guide, it's good when you can do it all. I started trail running a decade ago to supplement my skimo training. At first, I did only uphill racing. These days, I prefer technical trail running. We have everything in the Alps: flatter routes, and mountainous routes that take you up to glaciers. There's a lot to choose from. It's very different from other areas I've been to that might just have one type of trail running. You can even do high altitude trail running here. There are routes that will take you up to 4,000m! Right in Zermatt, I can run up and across the Hohlichtgletscher, to the summit of the Mettelhorn. That's 3,406m. You have big mountains here – you have to go up 1,000m just to get to that sense of flowing trails. In Zermatt, I know the trails well, but I still like to go up and explore.

I love the area around Goms, too. My girlfriend, Victoria, is from there. We do a lot of running around the Aletsch glacier. There, you have more of those really flowy trails. Trails like that, you get the same sense of rolling along as you do on a mountain bike. I like that a lot.

My favorite section of trail is the last 10km of the Ultraks race course, behind the Matterhorn, running down to Stafel and then climbing again. The trails there are beautiful, and they're great for all abilities. You overlook all of Zermatt. There are no lifts in sight. I really like it for that reason.

There's more I want to see. For example, the area of the Swiss Alps around Mont Blanc, Val Ferret and Champex. The Bernese Oberland area around Interlaken seems cool, too. There's still much more trail running in Switzerland I want to explore.

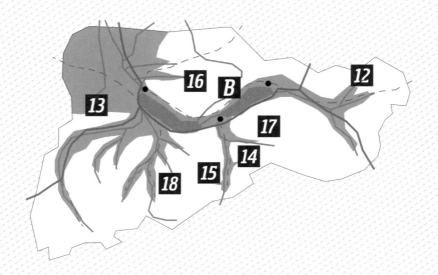

THE RUNS: BERNESE OBERLAND

Switzerland's Bernese Oberland is the highland region of the canton of Bern. It includes some of the most famous peaks in the Alps, including the Eiger, Mönch, and Jungfrau. Eight runs included in this book make their way through the Oberland.

Farming plays a large role in this German-speaking area. Most runs weave through herds of cows, sheep, and goats.

Thanks to thousands of kilometers of trails, the Bernese Oberland is a popular hiking destination for outdoor enthusiasts from around the world. The trails pass within sight of the region's five 4,000m peaks and through lush, green pastures. There is a wide array of private mountain huts, and dozens of others are managed by the Swiss Alpine Club. A number of long-distance hiking trails also pass through the Bernese Oberland.

The Bernese Oberland has an active trail running and racing scene. Most notable are the Eiger Ultra series each July, the challenging Inferno run up to the summit of the Schilthorn, the Mountain Man Ultra, and Glacier 3000 – a trail race that finishes with a final kilometer run across the Diablerets Glacier.

12

GENTAL
CRUISING THROUGH THE HEART OF SWITZERLAND

MAP

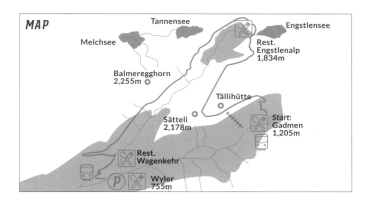

Tannensee

Engstlensee

Melchsee

Rest.
Engstlenalp
1,834m

Balmeregghorn
2,255m

Tällihütte

Start:
Gadmen
1,205m

Sätteli
2,178m

Rest.
Wagenkehr

Wyler
755m

PROFILE

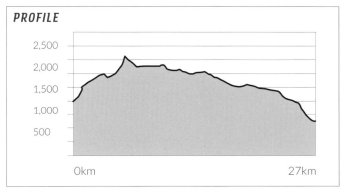

DIFFICULTY

PEAK SPOTTING
• Wendenstöcke
• Titlis

CANTON
Bern

OTHER CHARACTERISTICS
• Cables / Ladders: No
• Social media hero: No

DISTANCE 27km
ASCENT 1,126m
HIGHEST POINT 2,116m

STYLE
Flow 90%, Technical 10%

RUNNING
75%

COURSE
Point to point

ACCESS
• Parking: Innertkirchen,
  Wiler
• Bus: Gadmen
• Lift / Tram: Tällihütte

LET'S RUN!

Getting Started
Park at the Innertkirchen, Wiler Postbus stop and take the bus to Gadmen – or flip it. Either way, a short shuttle ride is necessary at the start or finish.

Both Gadmen and Wiler have services, so you can fuel up before heading for the hills. Passing through Gadmen, you'll soon pick up markings for the Bergweg, climbing through woods and ticking-off the main climb of the day's outing, nearly 900m.

High Traverse
With valley views below, herds of cows around and plenty of fountain fill-ups along the smooth trail, you'll be at Tällihütte before you know it. Take a break while enjoying the boxes of fresh herbs and the friendly hut dog.

A New View
More cruising leads to a sharp right, a steep climb to Sätteli col – and a whole new view. It's a great spot to soak in scenery on both sides of the pass before even more cruising. This time coasting down with Gental on your left, and then on to Engstlensee – a great spot for a dip. The trail takes you up to the hamlet of Engstlen and a brief run on a section of the Mountain Man trail race route.

Gental from the Other Side
Smooth trails lead you past farms, herds of cows and sheep, and finally from gravel to pavement. Watch for a sharp, unsigned left off the road, back to an old forest road. The Wanderweg leads you down to the valley, and day's end at Wiler.

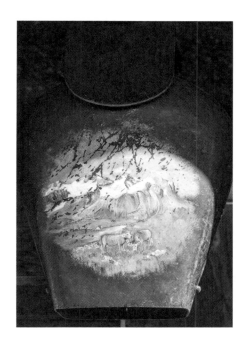

Why We Love It

This run is the very definition of a sweet cruiser. Long, easy sections of coasting will have you smiling, we guarantee it.

Not-to-be-Missed

Grab a *Nussgipfel* at the Tällihütte.

Easing Up

Skip the vert by taking the lift to Tällihütte. Then the run is almost entirely a downhill stride-out.

Pro Tip

We vote for parking the car at Innertkirchen, Wiler. It's easier to plan to catch the Postbus to the start than know when you'll be back at the end of the day.

Cheese Pilgrims

The Via Sbrinz, or cheese walk also passes through the Gental valley from Engstlenalp. Beginning in the middle ages, hard cheese from Central Switzerland was transported on these trails to markets in Domodossola, Italy. Today, a 110km marked path retraces the route.

MAP

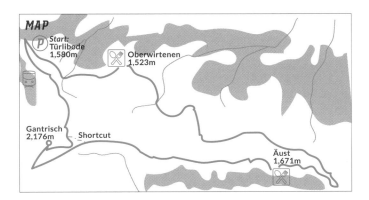

Start:
Türlibode
1,580m

Oberwirtenen
1,523m

Gantrisch
2,176m

Shortcut

Äust
1,671m

PROFILE

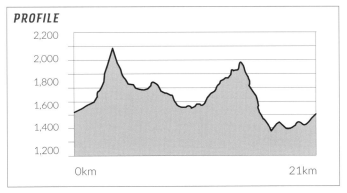

2,200
2,000
1,800
1,600
1,400
1,200

0km   21km

DIFFICULTY

DISTANCE   21km
ASCENT   1,239m
HIGHEST POINT   2,175m

PEAK SPOTTING
• Stockhorn
• Nünenenflue

PEAK TAGGING
• Gantrisch 2,175m

STYLE
Flow 90%, Technical 10%

RUNNING
75 – 100%

CANTON
Bern

COURSE
Loop, counterclockwise

OTHER CHARACTERISTICS
• Cables / Ladders: Yes
• Social media hero: Yes

ACCESS
• Parking: Türliböde
• Bus: Gurnigel,
  Wasserscheide

LET'S RUN!

Getting Started
The Gantrisch Nature Park, 400km² of forest, pasture, and mountain, sits between Bern, Thun and Fribourg, making it accessible from each of these cities. Here, the flat landscape suddenly rises to the peaks and ridges of the Prealps.

From your start near Wasserscheide, follow the dirt road between pastures, and past the Alphütte Obernünenen, an easy 2km warm up leads toward an impressive view of the mountains ahead. The angle begins to increase as you climb to Leiterepass.

On the Rise
Keep climbing from Leiterepass. Soon the trail splits to take a short out-and-back to tag Gantrisch peak before continuing on the loop. Reaching the summit is a bit technical with some fixed cables, but the effort is short. You'll reach the run's high-point only 3km after starting out. Back down to the split, descend to the saddle where the trail splits again.

Coasting Below the Crest
Instead of continuing to Schibespitz, drop from the col and settle in for a down-slanted traverse for 6km. Smooth trail hovers between the jagged ridgeline above and grazing grassland below while roaming through multiple alps along the way: Chuelouenen, Äust, and Stierehütte.

Next Up
The trail begins to angle upward to Oberi Walalp, and increases from the alp to reach Möntschelespitz and Homad. From the steep grassy slopes, you can see further into the Alps - white-capped mountains extending endlessly.

Closing the Loop
Follow signs towards Gurnigel Berghaus. The descent is steep, dropping you to more farms, Lägerlistand and Lägerli. After Salzmatte, 4km of dirt road lead you uphill to your finish, past the rolling Oberwirtnere Alpkäserei pastures decorated with rows of hanging cowbells, and the tiny Gantrisch Gurnigel ski station.

Why We Love It

Prealps with pointed peaks. Big mountain views and smooth running, set alongside farms, cows, sheep, goats, and clanging bells.

Not-to-be-Missed

A stop at one of the wooden Alpkäserei with window boxes overflowing with red geraniums. Besides cheese, the working dairies sell refreshments along the route.

Pro Tip

Run this loop in spring and fall. Aside from its two high-points, this run stays below 2,000m. The lower elevation makes it a good option early and late in the trail season when you can also avoid the tall grass and cow-trodden tracks in summer.

Getränke

Grab a farmer beer from the trough, and share a drink with the Jersey cows at Äust.

14

LAUTERBRUNNEN - GRINDELWALD

THE BEST OF THE JUNGFRAU MARATHON

MAP

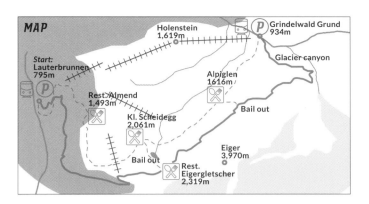

Grindelwald Grund 934m

Holenstein 1,619m

Start: Lauterbrunnen 795m

Glacier canyon

Alpiglen 1616m

Rest. Almend 1,493m

Bail out

Kl. Scheidegg 2,061m

Eiger 3,970m

Bail out

Rest. Eigergletscher 2,319m

PROFILE

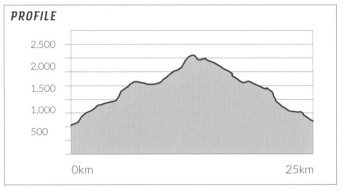

2,500
2,000
1,500
1,000
500

0km   25km

DIFFICULTY

DISTANCE	25km
ASCENT	1,678m
HIGHEST POINT	2,339m

PEAK SPOTTING
- Eiger
- Mönch
- Jungfrau
- Schilthorn

STYLE
Flow 80%, Technical 20%

RUNNING
50 – 75%

CANTON
Bern

COURSE
Point to point

OTHER CHARACTERISTICS
- Cables / Ladders: No
- Social media hero: Yes

ACCESS
- Parking: Lauterbrunnen Bahnhof
- Train: Lauterbrunnen, Grindelwald
- Lift / Tram: Multiple options (see map)

LET'S RUN!

Getting Started
There may be no more dramatic valley for an adventure than the steep-walled canyon that is home to Lauterbrunnen. Cowbells echo and waterfalls abound, including the 300m high Staubbach Falls. More than water plummets from the cliffs – Lauterbrunnen is one of the most active BASE jumping regions in the world. Over 15,000 jumps take place each year. It's a collision of idyllic Swiss charm and extreme mountain sports!

The Wall
This run doesn't have the easiest start, but does get you high quickly. Known as The Wall, the wide path from Lauterbrunnen up to Wengen begins at the train station and switchbacks its way up an infamous section of the Jungfrau marathon course. On race day, runners hear Pink Floyd's *Another Brick in the Wall* drifting through the trees, a sound indicating that Wengen isn't much further away.

Easing Up
At the Ryscher intersection, leave the Jungfrau course and follow the junction sign for Kleine Scheidegg to avoid the roads into Wengen that are used during the race. The next turns are marked by brown Mendelssohnweg signs as you follow a path named in honor of the 18th century composer who popularized the town. Stick to these lesser-used forest trails to traverse before rejoining the climb with marathon arrows just above Wixi. Trail-it up a little further and follow the moraine beside the Mönch and Jungfrau.

Changing Gears
Perched on the moraine, a boulder marks the Jungfrau Marathon's turn to Kleine Scheidegg. Instead of making that turn, finish the length of moraine to Eigergletcher. Weave through the station, now following the green markers for the Eiger Ultra Trail. Highlights of two great courses connected in one go!

Eiger Ultra Trail
Settle in for 7km of flowing low-grade downhill, half on the race route and half beyond to Lagerli. You can't help but lengthen your stride, jump, play, and speed along the buffed ribbon of trail unfolding along the base of the giant Eiger wall.

Ueli Steck

Coming Down
Careful! Above Alpiglen, don't make the hairpin turn to continue on the Eiger trail. Keep your flow in the direction of Gletscherschlucht to reach Lagerli. In the forest, descend and curve towards Grindelwald, ending at the Grindelwald Grund train station.

Why We Love It
Easy terrain, but big elevation gain for those of us who love going up! Dramatic, up-close views of some of the world's most iconic peaks. Plus, running on tracks of two notable Swiss races – and great stops along the way!

Wall of Fame
Not far from the Eigergletscher station, you'll find the handprints of famed mountaineers mounted on the base of the Eiger. Stop to press your palms into those of adventurers who tried their strength against the Mordwand, or 'Wall of Death.'

Cog Up
If you want less vertical gain, let the cog train to Wengen do it for you.

Pro Tip
In summer months and weekends, the Eiger trail can be crowded. Consider running the route on a weekday, or in early July or September/October. If it is busy, don't forget to give a polite heads-up when speeding past hikers!

Training Day
The trail and detours are well marked with yellow signs. There's no shortage of stops on or near the route, notably in Wengen, Kleine Scheidegg, and Alpiglen. If the day gets too long, a number of train stops from Kleine Scheidegg and Eigergletcher can take you down to Lauterbrunnen or Grindelwald.

15

STECHELBERG OBERSTEINBERG CLASSIC
A WORLD HERITAGE LOOP

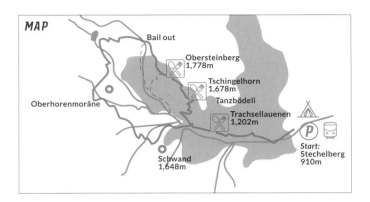

MAP

Bail out

Obersteinberg
1,778m

Tschingelhorn
1,678m

Tanzbödeli

Oberhorenmoräne

Trachsellauenen
1,202m

Schwand
1,648m

Start:
Stechelberg
910m

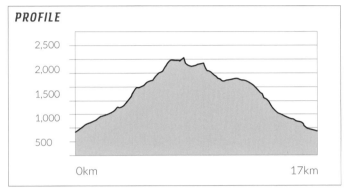

PROFILE

2,500
2,000
1,500
1,000
500

0km   17km

DIFFICULTY

DISTANCE   17km
ASCENT   1,371m
HIGHEST POINT   2,146m

PEAK SPOTTING
• Mittaghorn
• Grosshorn
• Breithorn
• Tschingelhorn
• Gspaltenhorn

STYLE
Flow 90%, Technical 10%

RUNNING
50 – 75%

COURSE
Loop, clockwise

CANTON
Bern

OTHER CHARACTERISTICS
• Cables / Ladders: No
• Social media hero: Yes

ACCESS
• Parking: Stechelberg bus stop
• Bus: Stechelberg Hotel

LET'S RUN!

Getting Started
Start running where the road splits at Hotel Stechelberg, and head up the valley on a wide gravel path. You'll feel the cool breeze of sinking cold air as you cross the foot-bridge over the Weisse Lütschine. Passing through Trachsellauenen, the run will begin its loop in the Unesco high country beyond Stechelberg.

Up to the Waterfalls
As you enter the woods, follow signs for Schmadrihütte where the trail reaches a 'T' junction at a fountain. The climb begins after crossing the river. First forest then pastures lead the way to Schwand. Take in the first of many big views of waterfalls, and peer across the valley to the high mountain inn on the left, Obersteinberg – a goal for later. Soon you're above the waterfalls as you enter the rocky alpine zone, and the Schmadri and Breithorn glaciers come into view. Look closely as you begin running again on this flatter terrain and you'll see Schmadrihütte on the skyline.

Cirque-tacular!
The flatter running comes with some rock hopping before you cross the river and climb to the day's high-point within the Oberhorenmoräne. Now, it's time to point 'em down, descending on winding single-track. You won't regret a pause by the Oberhoresee with views of glaciers and huge rock walls. Coasting past the grazing cows, you speed into Berghotel Obersteinberg.

Auto-Pilot
The trail running from Obersteinberg to the finish is some of the best of the day. Start by cruising on flowy single-track to Berggasthaus Tschingelhorn, where the miniature goats will likely distract you from your finishing pace. Switchback down pastures, through woods, and past farms. Don't want the day to end? Stop for milkshakes at Trachsellauenen. Don't worry about running on a full stomach, it's gentle gliding right back to Stechelberg.

Why We Love It
High in one of the most beautiful sections of the Berner Oberland, this loop traverses under and over dramatic waterfalls, past glaciers, and finally to one of the Alps' best known electricity-free 'candlelight' mountain inns, Obersteinberg. You'll find yourself stopping and staring at the sheer scale of it all!

Eye on the Sky
The Lauterbrunnen valley is one of the world's hot spots for BASE jumping and parapenting. For the inside aerial scoop, head to Airtime Cafe in Lauterbrunnen.

A Bit of History
Immediately after the parking lot above Trachsellauenen are the remains of a Middle-Age kiln, used to get iron and silver from ore. At one point, there were 18 buildings here!

Not-to-be-Missed
Ringed by the high peaks of the Breithorn, Tschingelhorn and Gspaltenhorn, stop for a rest by the Oberhornsee, a little-visited glacial tarn. It's remarkably peaceful. Careful – you could stay for hours!

Bonus
Run the out-and-back from Obersteinberg to Tanzbödeli, or 'The Dance Floor'. It's an improbable, grassy plateau with a stunning, 360-degree view that'll add 4.5km and 395m of vertical gain.

MAP

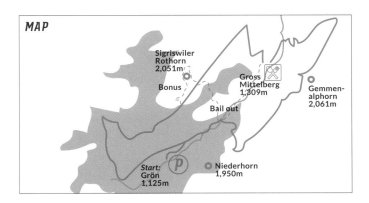

Sigriswiler
Rothorn
2,051m

Bonus

Gross
Mittelberg
1,309m

Gemmen-
alphorn
2,061m

Bail out

Start:
Grön
1,125m

Niederhorn
1,950m

PROFILE

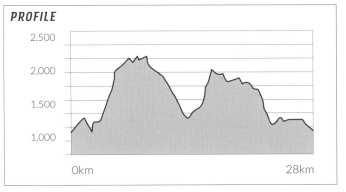

2,500

2,000

1,500

1,000

0km   28km

DIFFICULTY

DISTANCE   28km
ASCENT   2,067m
HIGHEST POINT   2,061m

PEAK SPOTTING
- Eiger
- Mönch
- Jungfrau

PEAK TAGGING
- Gemmenalphorn 2,061m

STYLE
Flow 60%, Technical 10%,
Exposure 30%

RUNNING
75%

CANTON
Bern

COURSE
Loop, counterclockwise

OTHER CHARACTERISTICS
- Cables / Ladders: Yes
- Social media hero: Yes

ACCESS
- Parking: Grön
- Bus: See transportation
  note
- Lift / Tram: Niederhorn

LET'S RUN!

Getting Started
Park at the large boulder in Grön, Beatenberg, and follow Justistalstrasse for 2km, along the trickling Grönbach to reach the alphorn bridge at Püfel.

Big Up
Just after crossing the bridge, watch for a wooden sign that's been spray-painted orange for the Bärenpfad. It's tucked into the edge of the forest. Here you make a sharp right to start the steep climb to Hohseil. Forested switch-backs lead to a series of ladders bolted to the limestone.

Ridge Time
Claiming the ridge, you're met with dramatic views of the Eiger, Mönch and Jungfrau. Turn away from the Niederhorn and run the ridge to Gemmenalphorn (2,061m), the day's high-point. When in doubt, follow the ibex – no one knows their way around the trails better!

Scoop
At Gemmenalphorn, you're looking at the ridge of the Hardergrat – a run for another day (p. 188)! From the far end of the loop, you'll see the length of the valley, leading towards Thunersee. Drop to Hindersberg and follow Justistalstrasse as far as Gross Mittelberg. Digging into the next climb, look for the bergweg up past Schäferhüttli to Schneide.

Single File
From the junction at Schneide, take the lower of two trails that traverses toward Schafloch. This airy single-track flows along the steep, exposed rock wall. The shelf is just wide enough to speed along. Pass the cave entrance at Schafloch and follow signs towards Sigriswil.

Winding Back
Still hugging the rock walls, tackle some technical forest trail until reaching Underbärgli's grassy pasture. Moments of sloping downhill through fields and farms give you a break from concentrating on your foot-ing. Don't tune out yet, though – there's a few technical switchbacks and a slight climb before joining the forest road and coasting back to Justistal, repeating only a short tail of road back to the start.

Why We Love It
Striding-out along high trails on both sides of the bucolic Justistal, you see where you're going and where you've been.

Transportation
Public transport is possible, but not easy. You can take a Postbus to the Niederhornbahn to access the first ridge, but it's a tough uphill finish to get to the Niederhorn lift at the end of the day. Check the timetables for last lifts.

Not-to-be-Missed
A stop to enjoy the view from the old chair-lift turned picnic bench at Hohseil.

In Bloom
Alpenrosen and plenty of wildflowers bloom in June. Gymnadenia rubra – Red Vanilla Orchid – a dark chocolate-scented flower, also grows on the grassy slopes. Pack a chocolate bar for cravings on the trail.

Say Cheese
In the fall, plan your run to visit the *Chästeilet* or cheese-sharing festival, when the cheese made collectively in the Justistal is divided among the farmers.

Pro Tip 1
Wait for snow to clear from the steep west-facing Bärenpfad.

Pro Tip 2
Watch the steep cliffs for groups of ibex.

Bail Out

Tired? At Gross Mittelberg you can follow Justistal-strasse back to the start. Save the other side of the valley for another day! Further along, the trail straight down from Schafloch is steep and slippery. A knee-pounding descent better avoided unless you really need to bail.

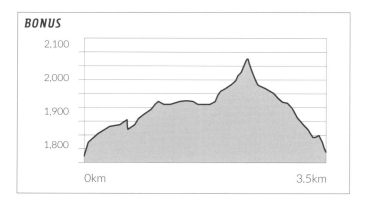

Bonus

Bring a headlamp and go through the 600m Schafloch tunnel! This natural ice cave was expanded to become a tunnel by the Swiss army. Once at the other side, you can spiral upwards to tag the Sigriswiler Rothorn, a 2,051m high peak, with a small scramble. Reconnect with the route following signs toward Sigriswil, adding 360m climb and 3.5km to the day.

17 SCHYNIGE PLATTE-GRINDELWALD

ABOVE IT ALL IN THE BERNESE OBERLAND

MAP

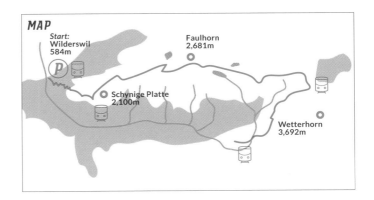

Start:
Wilderswil
584m

Faulhorn
2,681m

Schynige Platte
2,100m

Wetterhorn
3,692m

PROFILE

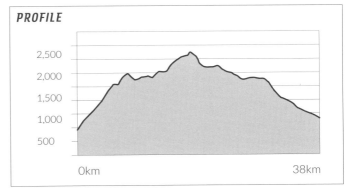

2,500
2,000
1,500
1,000
500

0km   38km

DIFFICULTY

DISTANCE	38km
ASCENT	2,340m
HIGHEST POINT	2,605m

STYLE
Flow 90%, Technical 10%

PEAK SPOTTING
• Eiger
• Mönch
• Jungfrau
• Hardergrat
• Wetterhorn

PEAK TAGGING
• Faulhorn 2,681m

RUNNING
75%

COURSE
Point to point

CANTON
Bern

OTHER CHARACTERISTICS
• Cables / Ladders: No
• Social media hero: Yes

ACCESS
• Parking: Wilderswil
  Bahnhof
• Train / Bus: Wilderswil /
  Grindelwald
• Lift / Tram: Schynige Platte
  cog train

LET'S RUN!

Getting Started

Beginning at Wilderswil, a valley gateway to the Jungfrau Unesco World Heritage Area, our run dispatches with the gain early on, leaving the rest of the day for soaking in some of the most famous views the Swiss Alps have to offer. There are plenty of stops for tasty calories, water – and chances to bail to a Grindelwald cafe if your legs decide to call it a day.

Pay Your Dues

Just a few minutes away from Interlaken in the heart of the Berner Oberland, here's a run that starts the moment you step off the train, right at the Wilderswil station. Follow signs for Schynige Platte, climbing steadily through pastures and switchbacking through woods. A few viewpoints tease as to what's ahead and you break into pastures with big views of the Thunersee and Brienzersee.

Race the Train

The climb continues under cliffs, past farms, and races the train to Schynige Platte. Soon enough, you're rewarded with views of a wide swath of the Bernese Oberland from the patio of the classic 1894 hotel at Schynige Platte.

Eye on the Eiger

Follow signs for Oberberghorn, then Faulhorn and First. You'll roll through pastures, twisting and turning with the terrain. Herds of cows with chiming bells provide a very Swiss soundtrack. Heading around Ussri Sägissa, the terrain becomes more challenging, with rockier footing on the way to Berghaus Männdlenen. Next, you'll climb towards the Faulhorn with cows, farms, and the well-known town of Grindelwald far below.

Tourist Time

A gravel track now offers some fast running alongside the Bachsee. In the summer, you'll dodge tourists from around the world. Before you arrive at First, swing right and run along the newly-constructed Cliff Walk that's bolted to the precipice. Watch your head on the rock outcroppings!

Farm Tour

From First, a combination of farm roads and single-track require your best slalom techniques to pass through herds of cows. Following signs for Grosse Scheidegg or Höhenweg 2400, you'll get expansive views of Kleine Scheidegg on the right, Meiringen on the left, and the looming Wetterhorn ahead. The Berghotel and restaurant offers a final chance for a pit-stop before the descent.

Scenic Single-Track

From the pass, quiet and narrow single-track leads you through rugged pastures, past ponds, and by some of the most scenic terrain of the day. Soon, the running becomes a bit more technical and steeper, crossing a bridge, then left at a sheep farm to a four-way junction. Turn on your GPS! It's time to follow the tracks for the final cruise into town. As much as possible, our route skips the busy paths and pavement. You'll follow unsigned local tracks past scattered chalets, old farm roads, a bit of a ski trail... then repeat as needed! Don't worry if you get off-route – nearly all paths lead to Grindelwald now. Just point your sneakers downhill and keep one eye on town. You'll run through the suburbs at this point - first Eggweid, Moos, then Mühlebach, before coasting into Grindelwald on Dorfstrasse.

A tip of our sweaty caps to you for ticking off a big run in the Berner Oberland. Time to kick back at *C und M*, or any one of the other great cafes and pubs in town!

Why We Love It
There may not be a run in this book with a higher percentage of flowing trails and big views! You'll be cruising much of the day with an eye on three of the most famous peaks in the world – the Eiger, Mönch and Jungfrau.

Save your Electrolytes
Happy to pass on the sweat-fest up to the treeline? At Wilderswil, hop aboard the 125-year old cog railway that climbs 1,420m to Schynige Platte so you don't have to!

Take it All In
After Männdlenen, consider a quick detour to the summit of the Faulhorn (2,681m) for the full 360-degree view.

Quads Toast?
Grab a lift at First, or a bus from Grosse Scheidegg to take you the rest of the way to Grindelwald if your gas is on 'E' or the weather threatens.

Pro Tip 1
Many of these trails can be busy in mid-summer. If possible, aim for a run mid-week or outside August vacations.

Pro Tip 2
Between Schynige Platte and Grosse Scheidegg, you'll be running sections of the Eiger Ultra's E101 and E51 trail races. The first edition took place in 2013. Since then, the race has grown to six events with over 4,000 participants, 500 volunteers and 100 staff.

MAP

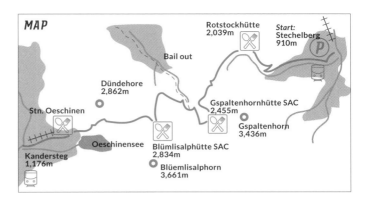

PROFILE

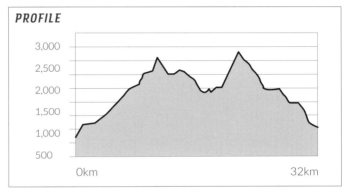

DIFFICULTY

DISTANCE	32km
ASCENT	2,999m
HIGHEST POINT	2,834m

PEAK SPOTTING
- Eiger
- Mönch
- Jungfrau
- Schilthorn
- Gspaltenhorn
- Blüemlisalphorn

STYLE
Flow 60%, Technical 30%, Gritty 10%

RUNNING
50 – 75%

COURSE
Point to point

CANTON
Bern

OTHER CHARACTERISTICS
- Cables / Ladders: Yes
- Social media hero: Yes

ACCESS
- Parking: Stechelberg / Kandersteg
- Bus/Train: Stechelberg / Kandersteg

LET'S RUN!

Getting Started
Stechelberg is a hamlet at the end of one of Switzerland's most dramatic valleys, the Lauterbrunnental. Your warm-up takes you along wooded switchbacks, across bridges, beside cascades, and across the Sefinen Lütschine.

Your Own Private Valley
Running along a single-lane gravel road through the tranquil Sefinental, you'll pass a rebuilt, water-powered saw mill. Easy footing allows you to take in the dramatic cliffs on your right. The road ends, and the first challenge begins, tackling a 630m gain to Rotstockhütte via pastures and some final rugged footing. Ready for a reward? We recommend the torte and a very fresh milkshake.

Into the Alpine Zone
After the hut, big pastures alternate fast-hiking with running that's less steep to take you into the land of rock and glacier. Final switchbacks take you to the famous Sefinafurgga. Take a few minutes at the bench just above the junction to say goodbye to the Lauterbrunnen valley and its summits: Schilthorn, Eiger, Mönch, and Jungfrau. Your view is about to change.

The Wilder Side
A scree-filled trail contours along an exposed slope with tricky footing (cables available) that soon gives way to easier cruising, past grazing sheep, and to one of the day's key stops: Gspaltenhornhütte. From there, you'll run down the spine of a lateral moraine of the Gamchigletscher and cross a gushing mountain tributary, using a fixed rope for security. Then, you reach another one of the day's highlights – crossing the icy snout of the Gamchi on a path that evolves as the glacier recedes. Slow down to follow the trail posts through loose, unstable terrain. Once across, you'll climb and turn a corner – to the sudden return of the green world.

Fuel Up for a Big Up

At the next junction, put your head down and don't look up. It's time to fast hike up 700m. Stairs and chains add novelty to the climb to Hohtürli, and the Blümlisalphütte welcomes you with fresh pie, tortes and other treats. Dramatically perched on a ridge between valleys, the Blümlisalphütte is one of the biggest Swiss Alpine Club huts.

Gravitational Payback

It's time to cash out all that hard work with one of the longest downhill cruises in this book – 1,656m of descent over 10.5km, to Kandersteg. You'll pass herds of sheep and cows at the Oberbärgli restaurant. Oeschinensee comes into view, but we'll stay higher, taking a wilder way, and skipping the tourist paths below.

As you approach town, the GPS track becomes invaluable. You'll follow the Bergweg signs for Kandersteg, passing through ski slopes, farm pastures and forests and finishing with a faint single-track down to Kandersteg. Mission accomplished – now grab that beer and soak those hammered legs!

Why We Love It
This is big-mountain running. Cross Sefinafurgga, and you're in the heart of the Bernese Alps. Trail running into Gspaltenhornhütte earns serious cred from mountaineers, surprised to see runners at the hut.

Not-to-be-Missed
Taking in the views, and the food, at Gspaltenhornhütte and Rotstockhütte, both great stops.

Pre-Run
Have a coffee at the Hotel Stechelberg, cross the bridge and top-off your water at the fountain next to the classic Alpenhof.

Bonus
Send your bags by SBB to Kandersteg, stay in town and make a weekend of it!

Pro Tip 1
Soak your tired quads in the Kander River that runs through town.

Pro Tip 2
This run requires a high commitment factor. Wait for the snow to melt on the big north-facing trail up to Blüemlisalphütte, go in fair weather, and take rested legs.

Lifts
Ride up to Mürren to cut early gain before making your way over to the route and take the lift from Oeschinen back to Kandersteg.

B HARDERGRAT
THE SWISS ALPS' AIRIEST RUN

MAP

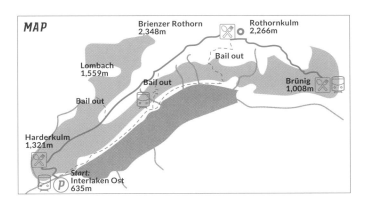

Brienzer Rothorn 2,348m

Rothornkulm 2,266m

Bail out

Lombach 1,559m

Bail out

Brünig 1,008m

Bail out

Harderkulm 1,321m

Start: Interlaken Ost 635m

PROFILE

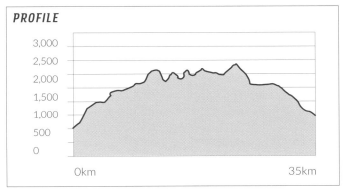

3,000
2,500
2,000
1,500
1,000
500
0

0km   35km

DIFFICULTY

DISTANCE   35km
ASCENT   3,286m
HIGHEST POINT   2,293m

PEAK SPOTTING
• Eiger
• Mönch
• Jungfrau
• Schreckhorn
• Finsteraarhorn

PEAK TAGGING
• Suggiture 2,084m
• Augstmatthorn 2,101m
• Gummhoren 2,040m
• Tannhorn 2,220m

CANTON
Bern

OTHER CHARACTERISTICS
• Cables / Ladders: Yes
• Social media hero: Yes

STYLE
Flow 50%, Technical 10%, Exposed 40%

RUNNING
50 – 70%

COURSE
Point to point

ACCESS
• Parking: Interlaken Ost / Brünig-Hasliberg Bahnhof
• Bus / Train: Interlaken Ost / Brünig-Hasliberg
• Lift / Tram: Harder Kulm / Brienzer Rothorn Bahn

LET'S RUN!

Getting Started

The Hardergrat has become a Swiss classic, well-known for its long grassy edge extending the length of the Brienzersee from Interlaken to the Brienzer Rothorn. The trail stays on the sharply defined ridge, unfolding intimidatingly far into the distance. Stunning views of the Jungfrau Region's highest peaks paired with cautious footing make for a long day on the trail, but one you won't forget.

Gain the Grat

Start up the forest trail, cutting steep switchbacks up to Harderkulm. By the time you break out of the trees, Interlaken and the Brienzersee have dropped far below. Stop to admire the view from the observation deck that cantilevers over the valley. As good as it is, the view only gets better throughout the run. The trail splits at the Harderkulm, directly behind and east of the restaurant. The high trail stays on the ridge while the lower option traverses flat and parallel with the trail from the Harderkulm station. If you follow the lower, flat option, you'll run a beautiful single-track trail for more than a kilometer before turning sharply up on a steep trail to join the ridge just before Höji Egg.

On the Edge

5km of ridge running later, you reach the Suggiture. From here, the length of the ridge stretches out, and for the first time, you see just how far you have to go. Keeping to the crest, you'll sawtooth up and over numerous grassy peaks, Augstmatthorn, Gummhoren, Tannhorn to name a few. Significant, airy drops on both sides keep you focused on the narrow trail beneath your feet. Hours pass and the ridge seems to be endless and even growing longer, until you reach Chruterepass. From the pass, angle along the backside of the ridge towards the Lättgässli staircase. Concrete steps signal the final bit of climb before a smooth traverse towards the Brienzer Rothorn.

All Downhill

From the Brienzer Rothorn station, one last climb of 100 meters gains the true Brienzer Rothorn summit before a trail splits off right for the Brünig Pass. This trail is nearly 100% smooth downhill running – the perfect finish to an incredible trail. Follow signs all the way down to Brünig pass where you can catch a bus or train to return to Interlaken.

Why We Love It

You balance on a narrow knife-edge ridge for nearly half the distance of this run, and as steep and crazy as it looks, much of the trail is runnable.

Trail Don'ts

Don't underestimate this route! The trail is slow going with plenty of physical and mental ups-and-downs. Don't go in wet weather – the grass is deadly slippery if wet.

Pro Tip

Carry poles and enough water for a long day. There is no water source for the entire length of the ridge from Harderkulm to the Brienzer Rothorn station.

Out of Steam

Be sure to know your options to bail even if you intend to power through the entire track. Have a plan to drop on either the south or north side of the ridge. One option is the Brienzer Rothorn funicular railway. It can save your knees 1,700m of descent and 12km, but it's an expensive way off the route. Check the schedule and start early from Interlaken if you want to catch the last train down to Brienz.

PORTRAIT

DIEGO PAZOS

Known for wearing a colorful bow tie at races, Diego Pazos is a force of nature. He transitioned from the soccer field to trails in 2011, and in the few years since, he's become one of Switzerland's most accomplished trail runners. He's stood on the podium or had top-10 results at races around the world, including Eiger Ultra Trail, Trail Verbier St-Bernard, CCC, UTMB and the 168km-long La Diagonale des Fous.

For the Lausanne native, however, trail running is much more than accumulating accolades. It's about building a sense of community and sharing the experience among friends. He is the driving force and Course Director behind one of the Alps' most popular new trail running events: the Montreux Trail Festival. "Trail running is very friendly," he says, "especially during long distances, we need to look out for each other when running. That's my philosophy."

Diego has an advanced degree in forensics and works for the Swiss Federal Police, coordinating the international exchange of information as they track organized crime. His wife Maya also trail runs, and together, they recently welcomed a baby boy, Kaylo, into their family.

© Compressport

The Prealps near Lausanne are my home trails. I grew up and still live in the region. Unlike many places in the higher Alps, you can start running in March and run until Christmas. It's not hard to get in a 1,000m climb, and the rocky, technical trails surprise a lot of people.

For me, it's all about having fun. I never get bored trail running in the Alps - the views change all the time and there's a lot of options. Trail running here is a game, and you are playing with stones, roots, steep climbs and big downhills. In just a few kilometers, you can run on a glacier, past a lake, through a forest, or summit a rocky peak.

One of my favorite runs starts by taking SBB to Montreux. I change and lock my clothes in the station before tackling a big, 1,600m climb. I run to the beautiful crest of the Dent de Jaman, then on to Rochers des Naye. The crest is very technical. It's true sky running with big views in all directions, from Lake Geneva to the Bernese Oberland to the Mont Blanc massif. On the way down, I can choose between a technical route or something easier.

Organizing the Montreux Trail Festival has been a lot of work for me and our team of ten on the Steering Committee. One thousand six hundred runners came to the first edition in 2017. It was emotional for me to see runners so happy. The Festival is truly an alpine event, with some challenging terrain and nice paths. It's great to be able to share them.

I also have a lot of personal projects I'd like to try – I like the idea of competition against oneself, and I really want to see Switzerland as a trail runner. Of course, I need to try to find a good balance with work, family, personal projects and racing. I would like to explore Graubünden and the national parks there. It looks so natural, wild and different from what I see here in this part of the Alps. Maya and I will be buying a family van soon, so, we can go there with Kaylo and camp. I'm looking forward to that.

You can find very nice things in every part of the world, but I love to come back to the Alps.

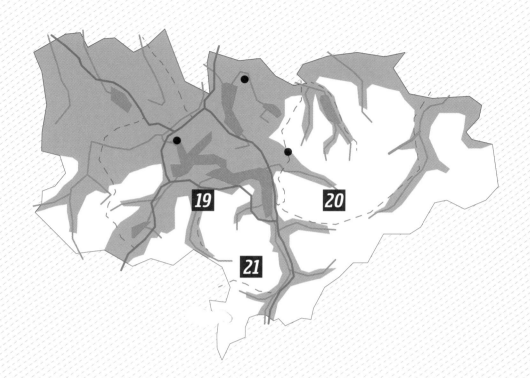

THE RUNS: CENTRAL SWITZERLAND

With smaller peaks that top out at 3,600m, the six cantons that make up Central Switzerland tend to be overlooked by mountain-goers, as they head for the bigger summits in the Valais or Bernese Oberland. But the region is filled with accessible mountain trails, and mountain towns that are a little quieter and less frequented. Easily within range of Switzerland's major cities, there's no lack of excellent trail running in the center of the country.

For our runs in this region, we've sought out the rugged, alpine terrain that is tucked away in Central Switzerland. Despite being a bit less vertical, there's a mixture of long, flowing traverses, alpine-feeling terrain, and even razor-like ridges that will add some vertigo to your vertical.

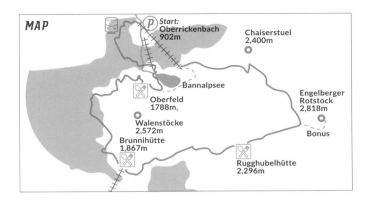

MAP

Start: Oberrickenbach 902m
Chaiserstuel 2,400m
Bannalpsee
Oberfeld 1788m,
Walenstöcke 2,572m
Engelberger Rotstock 2,818m
Bonus
Brunnihütte 1,867m
Rugghubelhütte 2,296m

PROFILE

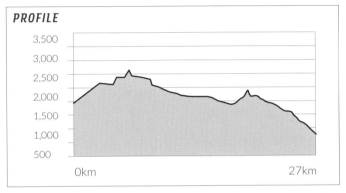

0km   27km

DIFFICULTY

DISTANCE   27km
ASCENT   1,499m
HIGHEST POINT   2,559m

PEAK SPOTTING
- Titlis
- Uri-Rotstock
- Brunnistock
- Gross Spannort

STYLE
Flow 80%, Technical 20%

RUNNING
75%

CANTON
Nidwalden

COURSE
Loop, clockwise

OTHER CHARACTERISTICS
- Cables / Ladders: Yes
- Social media hero: No

ACCESS
- Parking: Oberrickenbach Talstation
- Bus: Oberrickenbach Talstation
- Lift / Tram: Fell - Kreuzhütte

LET'S RUN!

Getting Started
Popular for hiking and skiing just south of Lake Lucerne, the Engelbergertal is a wide valley of alpine pastures and dairies. The run starts in Oberrickenbach, and loops around the impressive cluster of the Ruchstock, Spitz Mann, and Walenstöcke, through grassy slopes and rocky climbs.

Lift Off
Ride the aerial cableway from Fell up to Kreuzhütte to begin running near the Bannalpsee. Across the lake, you'll see the switchbacks to come down later in the day. Leaving the small station, signs point to Rot Grätli and Rugghubelhütte. Bells clang as you pass farms on the cow trails leading to the first col, Bannalper Schonegg (2,250m). Here, the grassy pastures shift to rockier terrain.

From Green to Grey
Runnable trail cuts through the scree and karst on the way up to Rot Grätli (2,559m). This col is the high-point of the run unless you're tempted to tag the Engelberger Rotstock, a bonus up-and-back before rejoining the route.

Down and Around
From Rot Grätli, a rolling downhill takes you to the Rugghubelhütte and traverses toward Planggenstafel. On the way toward Rigidalstafel, take the split at Holzstein on the higher trail to Brunni. Continue the traverse through the crowds that suddenly appear near the active Brunnihütte, until you reach Walenalp.

Back to Pasture
The last steep meters up to Walegg begin from Walenalp and stay beneath rugged towers. An inviting traverse pulls you towards the lake from a last high vantage. Drop down tight switchbacks to the Bannalsee, cross the dam, and follow signs to Eggiligrat and Oberrickenbach. Traverse a bit longer on the Wanderweg, then a steep forest descent leads to lower pastures, eventually returning to Fell.

Why We Love It
A diverse trail network with quick access to rugged, alpine terrain and long flowing traverses.

Not-to-be-Missed
Try the Sbrinz. The Swiss Parmesan made in this region is one of Europe's oldest cheeses.

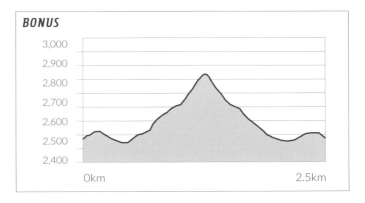

BONUS

(elevation profile: 2,400–3,000, 0km to 2.5km)

Bonus
Engelberger Rotstock (2,818m). The out-and-back adds 2.5km, 340m +/–, and a big panorama.

Pro Tip
There are plenty of huts along the route to refuel. No need to carry a heavy load of food or drink.

Extra
Too much for one day? Spend a night at Rugghubelhütte or catch the lift down from Bannalpsee.

Tickle Trail
Outside the Brunnihütte, you can wade in a shallow pond massaging your tired feet on gravel, wood, stones and in mud. Take your shoes off and make a quick lap around the Tickle Trail.

Felsenputzers
In 2009, Swiss Tourism created a parody video, recruiting for the fictitious Association of Swiss Mountain Cleaners. Felsenputzers were said to be responsible for the daily scrubbing of bird droppings from the rocks to keep the Alps beautiful. The April Fool's joke was made here in Brunni.

MAP

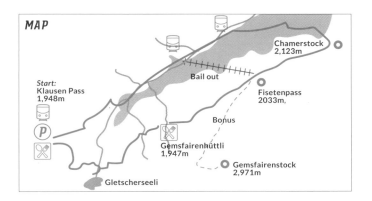

Chamerstock
2,123m

Bail out

Start:
Klausen Pass
1,948m

Fisetenpass
2033m,

Bonus

Gemsfairenhüttli
1,947m

Gemsfairenstock
2,971m

Gletscherseeli

PROFILE

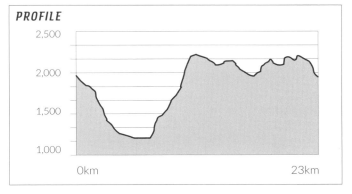

2,500

2,000

1,500

1,000

0km   23km

DIFFICULTY

DISTANCE   23km
ASCENT   1,110m
HIGHEST POINT   2,149m

PEAK SPOTTING
- Clariden
- Tödi

STYLE
Flow 80%, Technical 20%

RUNNING
75%

CANTON
Uri

COURSE
Loop, clockwise

OTHER CHARACTERISTICS
- Cables / Ladders: No
- Social media hero: No

ACCESS
- Parking: Klausen Pass
- Bus: Klausen Pass
- Lift: Urnerboden-
  Fisetengrat

LET'S RUN!

Getting Started
From Klausen Pass, follow signs toward Urnerboden (Via Alpina 1). The downhill comes first. You'll start with a rapid descent through pastures and forest trails occasionally crossing the switchbacks of the road. The 600m drop delivers you to the valley floor. Follow the grassy trail along the river for 4km of easy running.

Time to Climb
Choose the bridge before reaching Sonne to cross the Fätschbach. Follow signs to Wängi, up shaded forest switchbacks, cow pastures and short sections of dirt road. Fill up from the fountain at Wängi, and continue toward Chamerstock. Watch carefully as red and white paint leads to a steeper rise from the pastures to the ridge.

On the Ridge
Speed along the grassy Fisetengrat to Fisetenpass (2,036m). The trail continues along the grassy slope in a well worn line that is rolling, smooth, and dotted with picnic tables to take a break and enjoy the view across to the rock walls above Urner Boden.

Staying High
A short, technical descent angles through cow pastures and beside wild rock walls down to Gemsfairenhüttli. From the hut, you have a little climb on a trail more suited for hiking than running. Make a side trip to Gletscherseeli for a view of the glacial lake, and then a curving traverse before suddenly arriving back at Klausen Pass without a major downhill pound.

Early Bird
Local legend tells that the boundary between the cantons of Glarus and Uri was set by a footrace in the year 1315. At cockcrow, one runner would start from Altdorf and the other from Linthal, and where the runners met would settle the disputed boundary. The night before the race, Glarus overfed their rooster while Uri underfed theirs. The hungry Uri rooster crowed early, while the Glarus rooster overslept, allowing the Uri runner to cover the length of the Urnerboden before the Glarus runner had even begun his run. The Glarus runner then convinced the Uri runner to allow him to carry him back uphill as far as he could. The Glarus runner died of exhaustion while carrying the Uri runner. That spot marks the current border.

Why We Love It

A rare downhill start, quick kilometers along the river, a fast, grassy traverse, and the potential to add on a bonus peak with big views.

Not-to-be-Missed

At Fisetenpass, look in the drawer of the picnic table to find a poem about playing cards, drinking coffee, looking for deer, and writing your name in the register book. Follow the poem's advice and enjoy gazing across the valley.

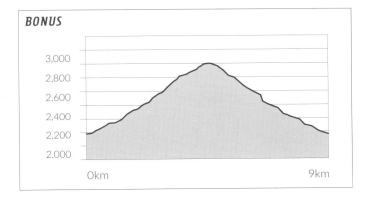

Bonus

Just a quarter kilometer past Fisetenpass, the rocky return trip to Gemsfairenstock (2,971m) adds 9km and 896m gain. Suddenly much more alpine, you'll feel far from both the traffic of the pass and the quiet green pastures. You're overlooking the Claridenfirn and big views of Tödi, Bifertenstock and Schärhorn.

Pro Tip

Save a little extra time for the section after Gemsfairenhüttli. For 3km, the trail requires a bit more attention to your footing.

SALBIT TRAVERSE
RUNNING THROUGH THE GRANITE GARDEN

MAP

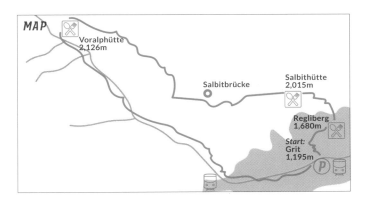

Voralphütte
2,126m

Salbitbrücke

Salbithütte
2,015m

Regliberg
1,680m

Start:
Grit
1,195m

PROFILE

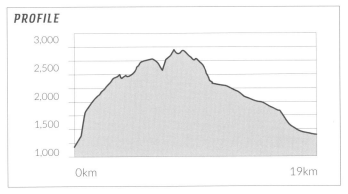

3,000
2,500
2,000
1,500
1,000

0km   19km

DIFFICULTY

DISTANCE   19km
ASCENT   1,680m
HIGHEST POINT 2,541m

PEAK SPOTTING
• Dammastock
• Galenstock
• Sustenhorn

STYLE
Flow 30%, Technical 40%,
Gritty 10%, Exposed 20%

RUNNING
50%

CANTON
Uri

COURSE
Loop, counterclockwise

OTHER CHARACTERISTICS
• Cables / Ladders: Yes
• Social media hero: No

ACCESS
• Parking: Grit, Göschenertal
• Bus: Göschenen, Grit

LET'S RUN!

Getting Started
The Salbit is known for razor-edge ridges and rock climbing; not fast, flowy trails. This loop promises to add some adventure to your run with steep climbs and vertigo inducing exposure.

Climb
From Grit, follow signs up the forest trail to Salbithütte passing Regliberg midway through this steep ascent. The stone Salbihütte with blue shutters is perched nearly 1,000m above the valley.

Chutes and Ladders
Hop onto the blue and white trail that connects Salbithütte and Voralphütte. The trail reaches the Salbitbrücke, a 90m long suspension bridge hanging over sheer rock walls that drop all the way down to the river valley. The trail continues to climb on the way to Voralphütte, crossing an exposed canyon fitted with a long series of ladders down and back up.

Rough Running
The jagged view matches the technical running, rock hopping, and rapid descent to Voralphütte.

Split Finish
From the hut, the trail becomes less steep and less technical, but still requires concentration. As you start out, choose your descent between the normal route or navigate the rockier footing on the north side of the river. The trails merge before Horefelli and follow the river for the final kilometers, lengthening your stride for an easy kick to close the loop.

Why We Love It
Steep up, technical down, big exposure, cables, ladders, and a swaying suspension bridge. Undoubtedly, it's an adventure.

Not-to-be-Missed
If your heart rate isn't already high from the vertical gain, look down into the gorge, Stotzig Chäle, while crossing the Salbitbrücke. Built in 2010, this suspension bridge connects the trails between the two high huts, Salbithütte and Voralphütte.

Caution!
The northwest facing gullies may hold snow and ice longer than expected. Don't risk it too early in the season. When you do go, hold on tight to the cables. This is no place to misstep.

Added Suspense
The connecting route over the bridge is maintained mid-June through mid-October when the huts are open. Other times use your own judgment.

Taking Care
2017 was the final year Hans Berger wardened the Salbithütte. For thirty-four summers, the climber took care of the hut, putting up forty of the sixty climbing routes on the walls above it, and initiated the building of the Salbitbrücke.

PORTRAIT

LIZZY HAWKER

Lizzy Hawker splits her time between the Swiss Alps and Nepal's Himalaya – on foot whenever possible. As an elite athlete, she held the world record for 24 hours on the road and won the Ultra-Trail du Mont-Blanc an unprecedented five times. Her passion for exploring has also led her beyond competition to Nepal and, twice now, she made a solo journey on foot, crossing the country from east to west on variations of the Great Himalaya Trail.

© Alex Treadway

I saw my first mountains, the Matterhorn and the 4,000m mountains of the Pennine Alps, on a visit to the Swiss Alps at the age of six. This was the beginning of a lifelong love of the mountains. That love plus an innate endurance and stubbornness led me from a career as a polar oceanographer to life as an ultra distance runner. Childhood dreams took me from the bleakness of suburban outer London, rows and rows of houses punctuated by car-filled roads, to the Swiss Alps and the Nepal Himalaya. The mountains were and are to me a wild and enticing landscape that gives a promise of a world to explore.

Switzerland is blessed with a magnificent network of trails that criss-cross its mountains. These paths, paired with the incredible Swiss transport system make all kinds of adventures possible. I love the feeling of freedom that comes with being able to find my way from A to B under my own steam, but it's an unassuming daily run that I treasure most. An easy trail, not long, not even really high … but the run I can do in the cool of the early morning, in the heat of the day, in the fading light of a setting sun, hard snow underfoot or heavy with the scent of late spring flowers.

As a runner I raced hard for a long time. Over those years, I often turned back to the mountains that first held my curiosity and passion as a child. The magnificent trails around the Monte Rosa on the Swiss-Italian border became my training ground.

Over time, though, priorities change and focus shifts. For a long time, racing challenged me, taught me a huge amount, and gave me the opportunity to explore. Now it's time to share that joy with others. This is the motivation for the race Richard Bull and I have created together - the Ultra Tour Monte Rosa. The first edition of the 100 mile Ultra Tour was held in 2017. For years, I've been thinking this route would be great

for a race. To finally see it happen was both very special and almost unreal - the result of the hard work of a few people over many years. It's a tough route that lives up to its description - bold, brutal and beautiful. To see people crossing the finish line having gone beyond what they thought they could do, both humbled and strengthened by their experience, makes all our work worthwhile. We also have a 4-day stage race over the same route and training camps throughout the summer. The latter are a hard training, perfect endurance preparation for long races, but they are also four days of companionship in a wonderful mountain environment.

For me the Swiss Alps is still a treasure trove of mountain trails to explore, whether alone or in the company of friends. For now, long challenges such as Fastest Known Times and sharing mountain journeys with like-minded people draw me more than competition does. I look forward to just soaking up the beauty of the mountains and helping others do so, too!

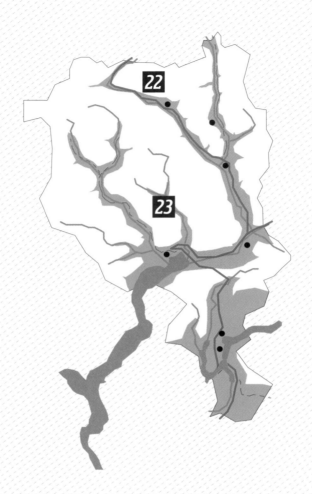

THE RUNS: TICINO

Switzerland's Ticino region is a trail running gem – remote, peaceful, sparsely populated. The Italian-speaking canton hosts a network of trails that remain very much off the beaten path. Just two of our runs take place here, but there are countless other trails to be explored.

Ticino is the southernmost canton in Switzerland. The region offers the best of both Switzerland and Italy - Switaly. Nicknamed "Switzerland's Sun Porch", temperatures are closer to those of its southern neighbor, but with a remarkable network of Postbuses to reach far into the remote valleys. Though Ticino's weather is sunnier and warmer than the rest of Switzerland, the canton also has a perilous meteorological claim to fame: it has more lightning strikes than anywhere else in Europe.

Head to Ticino early in the trail running season to avoid the lingering snows elsewhere in the Alps. In midsummer, when tourists are flocking to Zermatt and Grindelwald, the trails of Ticino will still be relatively tranquil – often populated more with sheep and ibex than with hikers.

MAP

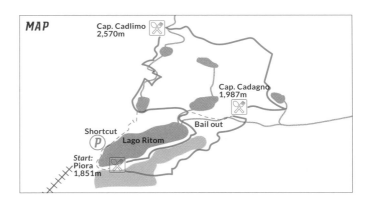

PROFILE

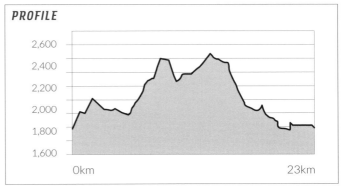

DIFFICULTY

DISTANCE   23km
ASCENT   1,455m
HIGHEST POINT 2,571m

PEAK SPOTTING
• Piz Medel
• Scopi

STYLE
Flow 70%, Technical 30%

RUNNING
75%

CANTON
Ticino

COURSE
Loop, counterclockwise

OTHER CHARACTERISTICS
• Cables / Ladders: No
• Social media hero: No

ACCESS
• Parking: Piora
• Bus: Piotta (base of funicular)
• Lift / Tram: Piora Funicular Railway

LET'S RUN!

Getting Started
Blending traditional cowbell-clanging Swiss countryside with Italian colors and energy, Ticino offers the best of both. Along the trail, this run transports you to somewhere even farther away. It picks you up and drops you into Tibet or Nepal. The usual grazing cows are replaced by distinctly shaped yaks and the bells sound more melodic, like singing bowls. Welcome to Shangri-La. The terrain is rocky, tougher and imprinted with deep lakes and fingers of streams.

Rolling Out
From the high parking at Piora, pass through the Ristorante Lago Ritom to a cluster of trail signs. Follow the one pointing to Pinett. The trail climbs gradually through low scrub and blueberry bushes, and the first couple hundred meters of gain pass at an easy trot. From the intersection at Pinett, turn left towards Cadagno. A rolling traverse carries you through the Val Piora before a short drop into the valley meets the road to Capanna Cadagno for a few hundred meters.

Up and Over
A sharp right at Capanna Cadagno starts your climb to Capanna Cadlimo. Reaching a wide grassy ridge that overlooks multiple lakes, you meet a blue and white painted trail to continue steeper uphill. From the pass above Laghetti della Miniera, you cross a wild, rocky, and flattish plateau before dropping to the river crossing.

Tibet in Ticino
Rock hopping across the river, you join the red and white trail winding up to Capanna Cadlimo. Passing through the herd of yaks, waving prayer flags, and above a shepherd's residence made of stone, you'll imagine you have wandered from the Alps into the Himalaya.

Coming Down
Large arrows for Ritom are painted on a rock to begin the descent from Cadlimo. The trail is technical but playful as you rapidly lose meters between Punta Negra and Lago Scuro. It's tempting to stop at the shore beside Lago di Tom before rounding the water's edge. A short climb followed by a smooth slant takes you to the Cadagno di Fuori. Turn right on the road and watch for a quick left onto the trail that overlooks Lago Ritom.

Lakefront Finish
Signs to Piora/Staz bring you back. Drop to Lago Ritom and curve around it. Save your kick for fast-running through rolling forest, and don't forget to peep through the trees at the glistening water.

Why We Love It
Lakes, waterfalls, prayer flags, yaks... it's like being far away without traveling far at all.

Not-to-be-Missed
Watch for herds of chamois on the cliffs, and marvel at the many deep blue lakes.

Pro Tip
Run this in fall for the changing yellow larch, golden grasses, and fiery-red blueberry bushes.

Follow the Sun
The area between Lukmaier Pass and the Valle del Sole is especially sunny, even for sun-filled Ticino.

Formaggio
Ticino produces more different types of cheeses than any other canton in Switzerland. Try the Formaggio d'Alpe Piora, the most notable from the region. The herbs, flowers and grasses growing in the high pastures where the cows graze aren't found anywhere else.

Pass Fact
The Lukmanier Pass is the only north-south passage through the Swiss Alps that doesn't exceed 2,000m. It's low altitude means it stays open for travel through the winter.

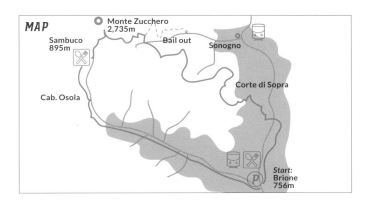

MAP

Monte Zucchero 2,735m

Sambuco 895m

Bail out

Sonogno

Corte di Sopra

Cab. Osola

Start: Brione 756m

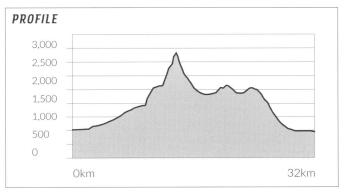

PROFILE

3,000
2,500
2,000
1,500
1,000
500
0

0km   32km

DIFFICULTY

DISTANCE 32km
ASCENT 2,607m
HIGHEST POINT 2,733m

PEAK SPOTTING
- Pizzo Campo Tencia
- Corona di Redorta
- Triangolino
- Cristallina
- Madom Gröss

PEAK TAGGING
- Monte Zucchero 2,735m

CANTON
Ticino

OTHER CHARACTERISTICS
- Cables / Ladders: No
- Social media hero: No

STYLE
Flow 50%, Technical 20%, Gritty 30%

RUNNING
75%

COURSE
Loop, clockwise

ACCESS
- Parking: Ristorante Piee
- Bus: Brione (Verzasca), Piee

LET'S RUN!

Getting Started
Located in the Valle Verzasca of Ticino, this is a wild run in a quiet region of the Alps. Over centuries, invading armies largely left residents alone to farm because of its isolated location. Traditional, gray rustici, or stone farm houses, still dot the hillsides.

Along the Osura
From Piee, start up the road and bear left passing farms and a small cheese and honey stand, crossing a pedestrian bridge after the first kilometer. If you have to run on a road, this is the one! Gaining a few hundred meters with the rapids of the Osura River on your left and centuries-old rustici on your right, it's one of the coolest roads to run in the Swiss Alps. Take time to look up, too – huge waterfalls tumble down the valley walls. The road turns to gravel, then single-track. You'll cross the Osura after 6km, near the cluster of houses known as Vald.

The Valley Narrows
Across the river, you'll alternate climbing with running. There's beautiful single-track here, through rough pastures and pine forests, stretching to the Capanna Osola, a quiet self-service refuge not far from the end of the valley. After a short section of rugged pasture, turn left and climb. It's head-down time as you grind out some vert! Contour around the valley, now above the trees and soon above the waterfalls. Rifugio Sambuco comes into sight – another welcome respite. Water is available, but treating is recommended here, or you can go for the honor-system soda, coffee, or even wine!

Up to Big Views
After Sambuco, you'll climb steeply through rough pastures. Goats roam this high terrain as you make the rocky ascent to the Bocchetta di Mügaia at 2,518m. With two hundred meters of easy scrambling from the col, you reach the summit of Monte Zucchero, a beautiful pyramid-shaped mountain. Summit tagged, scramble down technical terrain. Passing a shepherd's hut, you'll continue descending through grassy switchbacks to Brüsoo. Look up to dramatic waterfalls and the enormous basin above - then glance down to Sonogno, a village of only eighty-seven residents, that dates back to the 1200s.

Contour Tour

A long stretch of high-mountain cruising unfolds through two large basins. Ibex, not used to trail runners, will dart away before you see them. You'll pass centuries-old stone shepherd huts, some still in use. The terrain alternates luxurious grassy cruising with rock hopping up and down small rises. While rolling, it's still challenging.

Coming Down

From the junction at Corte di Sopra, let gravity take over. Once through the goat pastures, you'll drop rapidly along forested trails to the hamlet of Gerra.

Valley Cruising

Pass through the few houses that make up Gerra, cross the road and then the Verzasca River by footbridge. Then cruise beside the river on a wide path, passing through the hamlet of Alnasca, and finally cross the river one last time. It's been a wild and rugged route through one of Switzerland's remotest valleys. The time is now beer-thirty at Ristorante Piee!

Why We Love It

Want a break from tourists and cable cars at every turn? This is your run! It doesn't get much more remote or wild feeling in the Alps. You might even have Monte Zucchero to yourself. Despite being the second-highest in the region, it's less often summited than nearby peaks.

Park and Run

Parking across from Ristorante Piee – a Verzasca Parking Card is required and can be purchased 400m up the road.

Pro Tip

Avoid the dreaded bonk! There's no food available en route, so stock up for a full day out.

Don't Be Lunch

Descending from Corte di Sopra, you can quickly bomb down pastures near Vèld and into guardian dogs with a taste for trail runners. If the dogs are working in this area, don't make eye contact and keep 300m away from the herd.

What's the Rush?

Verzasca is a special area. Make a long weekend of it and fast-pack to one of the ultra-quaint self-service huts along the route. Or stay in the valley and tick off a second run!

PORTRAIT

JULIA BLEASDALE

Julia Bleasdale lives in Pontresina, a mountain town in Switzerland's Engadine region. The Alps have been a part of much of this British-German trail runner's life. Her parents met on a peak in Austria's Stubai valley, and Julia would later spend her childhood summers in the country's Sellraintal south of Innsbruck.

In 2008, a friend introduced her to the Engadine, and Julia fell in love with the valley during her summer training there for the 2012 London Olympics. Four years later, the Engadine became her home. Julia says: 'Taking part in the Olympics was a career highlight, but it's here in my beloved Alps that I feel true harmony and connection.'

Today, she runs through the mountains and forests of the Engadine and shares that passion with others, both on the trail and by developing running opportunities in the region.

© JB

One day in 2013, I was running up Val Roseg along a winding woodland path. A big vista with glaciated peaks suddenly opened up in the distance. There was a gushing stream nearby and the echo of cowbells. At that point I knew I'd have to be in the Alps and that this was the place. I had found home once more.

The distinctive scents of the alpine meadows and pine trees help me to find peace and contentment, to run and explore. It just feels ingrained. I feel a strong connection to the alpine setting here, its culture and the way of life.

The Alps have many beautiful locations, but what is unique about the Engadine is its great diversity. There are flat gravel trails, lakeside paths, rolling terrain through pine forests, rugged peaks and open valleys with a variety of directions to take. There are endless running possibilities in this wilder, quieter part of the Alps. You'll find hidden hamlets, less traversed side valleys and crystal lakes high up on the mountainside. In the shoulder seasons, you can drop down into Italy, rapidly descending 1,000m in elevation to find yourself in a different season!

One trail I love to run is the Röntgenweg, a zigzag path that starts at Pontresina's church, Santa Maria, and ascends through a pine forest before heading towards the Paradis Hut. You can lose yourself in thought on the trail, unless the ibex are out and about! Then, suddenly, you find yourself in open mountain pasture with fantastic views of the Bernina Massif. Climb further towards the Paradis Hut and the views just get better and better!

As a professional athlete, you always have to be careful with your time and stay focused. It can be a lonely existence. I am at a point in my career where I feel driven to be innovative and creative, while sharing trail running in the Engadine with others. I'd like to use my experience from traveling, training and competing around the world to grow a trail running community and enable many others to enjoy the special qualities of this region.

Everyone seeks his or her own sense of purpose, satisfaction and happiness. I'm asking myself, 'What can I give?' Here in the Engadine, I have a fresh direction and I am excited to go for it!

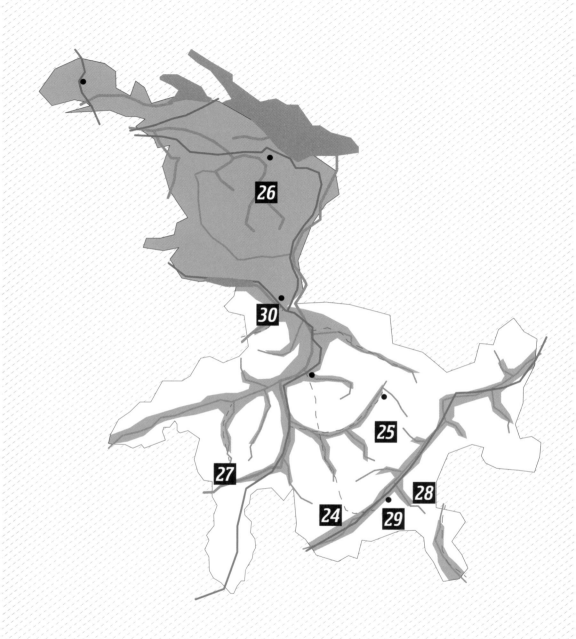

THE RUNS: EASTERN SWITZERLAND

A little harder to access, Eastern Switzerland has retained a wild, untamed feel. Getting there often requires an extra effort – particularly in the Engadine area – and that makes all the difference. Trails roll through pastures and over cols free of most of the infrastructure that is omnipresent in much of the rest of the Alps. Many of the peaks are lower than their Berner and Valais neighbors, with just one peak, Piz Bernina, over 4,000m. But they are no less beautiful.

Eastern Switzerland is a vast region, stretching across nearly 200km. It is less densely populated, with small villages providing hospitality and a chance for resupply. Graubünden is the country's largest canton, and shares borders with Italy, Austria, and Liechtenstein. The area is so large, it has three official languages – Swiss German, Italian and Romansh.

If there is an epicenter for trail running here, it's Pontresina at the base of Piz Languard, which is easily within striking distance of five of the runs in this book. When in Eastern Switzerland, leave enough time to enjoy *Nusstorte*, a regional nut and honey pie, when your run is done.

MAP

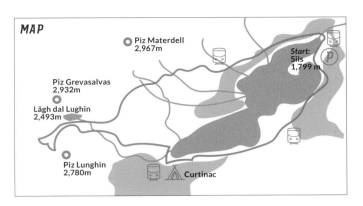

Piz Materdell 2,967m

Start: Sils 1,799 m

Piz Grevasalvas 2,932m

Lägh dal Lughin 2,493m

Piz Lunghin 2,780m

Curtinac

PROFILE

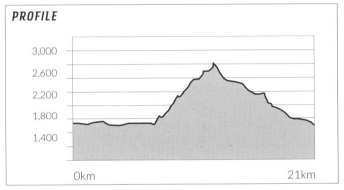

3,000
2,600
2,200
1,800
1,400

0km   21km

DIFFICULTY

DISTANCE   21km
ASCENT   1,051m
HIGHEST POINT   2,780m

PEAK SPOTTING
- Piz Duan
- Cima dal Cantun
- Piz Corvatsch
- Piz Roseg
- Piz Bernina

PEAK TAGGING
- Piz Lunghin 2,780m

STYLE
Flow 70%, Technical 20%, Exposed 10%

RUNNING
75%

COURSE
Loop, clockwise

CANTON
Graubünden

ACCESS
- Parking: Sils
- Bus: Sils/Segl Baselgia stop

OTHER CHARACTERISTICS
- Cables / Ladders: No
- Social media hero: No

LET'S RUN!

Getting Started
Easily accessible from St. Moritz by Postbus, the stone-built houses in the quiet 500 resident village of Sils-Maria feel distant from the posh shops of its internationally-known neighbor. Our run starts at the edge of Silsersee. If you need supplies, there are a few shops in Sils/Segl, and water is available at the fountain in the village center.

Coast Along the Coast Warm-up
For a gentle warm-up, coast around Lej Segl along rolling terrain, moving from shore to forest and back. Enjoy a morning *Milchkaffee* at Isola, with two cafes and a fountain for topping off your water if you'd like to start light.

Upward Bound
It's time to leave the flat behind and get into the mountains! Run a short access road around the end of Lej Segl, cross the highway, and kick-off your vert for the day. You'll fast hike some of the climb. Early on, bear left at a bench, where an unsigned path comes in from the right. Smooth switchbacks lead up to more challenging sections with loose rocks underfoot, until you reach the high alpine Lägh dal Lunghin. Ringed by Piz Lunghin and Piz Grevasalvas, it's a beautiful stop.

Summit Loop
The loop up to Piz Lunghin from the lake only makes up 3km and 300m gain but adds a little technicality and exposure to an otherwise gentle run. The trip up takes you near the Pass Lunghin, a rare triple watershed. From here, water flows in three directions – towards the Atlantic (via the Rhine), towards the Mediterranean (via the Po) and towards the Black Sea (via the Danube). Trickle back down to Lägh dal Lunghin.

Leaving Lägh dal Lunghin
Time to leave this wild-feeling area and settle down. You'll start with fast running, contouring around a ridge to a tiny alpine tarn near the summit of nearby Muotta Radonda, then down through a miniature alpine ravine.

Hello Heidiland

Pass through the marshy flats at Plaun Grand, keeping an eye out for faint paint on the rocks, then descend through pastures as the trail widens. Here, you're above the tiny hamlet of Grevasalvas. Across the way, take in the views of the peaks that mark the border with Italy: Piz Roseg and Fedoz, Cima di Rosso and Cima di Castello among others.

Rolling Down

At the junction, tighten your laces and get ready for a fast cruise to the finish! Gentle downhill terrain over pastures, across scree slopes and through the larch forest make for some of the best trail running of the day. Add in the view of Silsersee on your right, and we promise you'll be smiling when gravity lands you back on the shore.

Why We Love It

This is the perfect mellow run (summit aside) in the Engadine. No sustained super-tough climbs, yet it offers a wild mountain feel.

You'll Get Teary-Eyed

Interrupt the return by dropping 80m and a hundred years to Grevasalvas. This tiny village is worth the out-and-back, but you may not want to leave. When we ran past, alphorns lured us down to the stone and wood houses to drink from the trough and sit in the sun. Apparently, others like the spot too, because Grevasalvas was the setting for the 1978 remake of the movie *Heidi*. Producers settled on it after visiting dozens of hamlets in the Swiss Alps.

Sail Away

Want to shorten your run and add some decadence? Lake Sils is home to the highest scheduled boat service in Europe, courtesy of Franco Giani, who looks the part of a grizzled sea captain. He'll tell stories as he crosses the lake, with stops at Sils Maria, Chastè, Plaun da Lej, Isola and Maloha. For 40 years, he's been sailing from June through September. To book a trip to or from any one of several points on the lake, see *www.sils.ch*.

Pro Tip

Run this one in late June or early July and you'll be running through fields of primroses, blue gentians and other alpine flowers, just blooming. If you find yourself singing like *Heidi*, don't worry – you probably won't be the only one. It also glows with golden larch in the autumn. There's no bad time to be here.

Fun Fact

Heidi wasn't the only movie filmed on the route of today's run. Clouds of Sils Maria was filmed throughout the area – up high near the lake, and in the village as well. The lesbian romance drama competed for the prestigious Palme d'Or in the 2014 Cannes Film Festival.

MAP

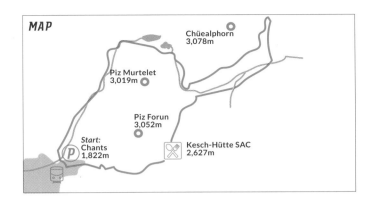

Chüealphorn
3,078m

Piz Murtelet
3,019m

Piz Forun
3,052m

Start:
Chants
1,822m

Kesch-Hütte SAC
2,627m

PROFILE

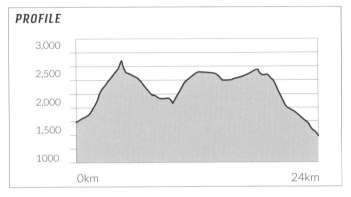

3,000	
2,500	
2,000	
1,500	
1000	

0km   24km

DIFFICULTY

DISTANCE   24km
ASCENT   1,370m
HIGHEST POINT   2,630m

PEAK SPOTTING
- Piz Kesch
- Piz Vadret
- Chüealphorn

STYLE
Flow 80%, Technical 10%, Exposed 10%

CANTON
Graubünden

RUNNING
75%

COURSE
Loop, counterclockwise

OTHER CHARACTERISTICS
- Cables / Ladders: No
- Social media hero: Yes

ACCESS
- Parking: Chants
- Bus: Chants. Daily, but infrequent

LET'S RUN!

Getting Started

Chants is a cluster of about twenty homes and, thankfully, the Berghaus Piz Kesch Cafe, if you need to fuel up. You'll pass several water fountains right in town. Follow signs toward Kesch Hut to pass through Naz and a sharp turn from Chamarchet starts you up forest switchbacks. Before you know it, you're in an open high valley with mountains on either side and straight ahead. You'll make your way around Piz Forun and Piz Murtelet.

The High Country

You're now entering a dramatic, high glacial cirque with moraines and cold streams constantly cutting new courses. Kesch-Hütte can be seen against the skyline. The hut is modern yet cozy, and well worth a refueling stop. Your route continues on the other side of the hut, descending with easy running to a junction below.

Sweet Single-Track

Running through the broad, wild Val Funtauna, footing is easy. You can run and take in the enormity of this remote valley of the Engadine at the same time. On your left, up high, is your return route. For now, head down to the farmhouse in the distance, swing left and climb into the still wilder Ils-Craunzs Valley. You'll be fast hiking, or running if you've got energy to burn.

We Can Be Heroes

From the high junction, hairpin-turn left to begin your return, following signs toward Lai da Ravais-ch. This is hero running at its best, but keep one eye on your feet because the trail is narrower and more rugged. Contouring high above the Val Funtauna, the trail's just exposed enough for a few 'Oh wow' moments... without inducing knee-knocking fear. Kesch-Hütte comes back into view, as you head uphill towards the Ravais lakes. Take a break to cool your toes or jump in the glacial water. We dare you!

Giddy Gliding

There might not be a trail run in this book with a more pleasant finish. The speed-inducing easy downhill only gets smoother and grassier, with steep-walled pastures on each side. The run finishes by passing Scottish Highland cattle as you coast by farmhouses into Chants.

Why We Love It
If we had to pick one run that best represents the Engadine, this would be it. Wild, remote, yet accessible. The Engadine has a vibe all its own, and that feeling comes through in spades on this run.

Pro Tip
Go in the fall when the cows are gone and colors are golden.

Beware of Dog
This run passes through large grazing areas for sheep – remember that as you step over the fences, you're in a guardian dog's space.

Sending Out an *SOS*
There's no cell signal, so don't be expecting to answer emails or text. There are, however, boxes with old-school emergency phones inside.

Bonus
Nearing the back of the Ils Craunzs Valley, it's just ten minutes to Scalettapass, and well worth the out-and-back for a jaw-dropping view of the Dischma Valley. If it's cold or wet, the rustic Schutzhütte Scalettapass shelter awaits, just out of sight.

Hupp, Hupp, Hut
Feeling like a night out? Spend it at Kesch-Hütte, and you'll have better odds of making the final Chants Postbus departure.

Say What?
In 2017, Bergün announced a ban on tourists taking photos of the beautiful village. "It is scientifically proven that beautiful holiday photos on social media make the viewer unhappy," joked the village's tourist office, "because they cannot be there themselves."

MAP

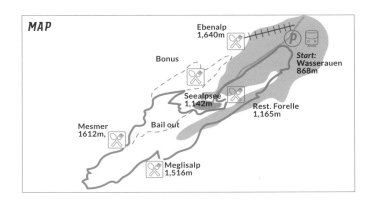

Ebenalp
1,640m

Bonus

Start:
Wasserauen
868m

Seealpsee
1,142m

Rest. Forelle
1,165m

Mesmer
1612m,

Bail out

Meglisalp
1,516m

PROFILE

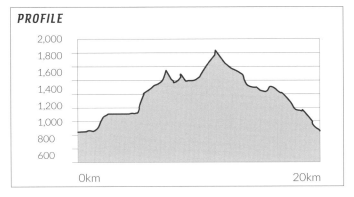

DIFFICULTY

DISTANCE	20km
ASCENT	1,622m
HIGHEST POINT	2,074m

PEAK SPOTTING
- Säntis
- Hoher Kasten

STYLE
Flow 80%, Technical 10%,
Exposed 10%

CANTON
Appenzell Innerrhoden

RUNNING
75%

OTHER CHARACTERISTICS
- Cables / Ladders: Yes
- Social media hero: Yes

COURSE
Loop, counterclockwise

ACCESS
- Parking: Gasthaus
  Alpenrose
- Bus / Train: Wasserauen
- Lift / Tram: Ebenalp, cuts a
  few meters of vertical – but
  adds running distance

LET'S RUN!

Getting Started
The Alpstein is a magical place – a hidden range with huts and berghauses in the most improbable locations. It's a trail running roller coaster – up, down and around rocky fins, cols and cliffs. Around every corner is a new and unexpected view.

Wasserauen, the access point, is a busy trailhead with every amenity you could want: easy transport, parking, water and food at several locations.

Take a Bow
This first section is popular with older walkers and families, so expect to get some curious looks – and a bit of clapping – as you grind through a series of short, steep hills. At the Gasthaus Forelle, swing left to run around Seealpsee. It's impossible not to stop here to take a photo with the valley walls, narrow Fehlalp ravine, and Säntis all in view.

Earn the View
Leaving the valley at Seealpsee junction, climb steeply for 400m. There are plenty of cables to lend a hand. You'll break above the trees to a steep pasture with big views. A few traverses later, you'll be enjoying a break at Altenalp, where you can refill your water and watch Bruno and Gerlinde Neff-Stäbler make cheese.

The Alpstein roller coaster starts here – you'll soon top out at a narrow col then plummet steeply to Berggasthaus Mesmer, a great spot for coffee or even a full plate of Rösti.

Head into the steep and narrow ravine of Fehlalp... then fast hike your way out on a switchbacking cabled escape. A final push up a technical scree slope, and you're over another hump, into entirely different territory at the day's high-point, 2,074m high Wagenlücke.

Big Views
A fast descent from the pass features technical rock hopping interspersed with smooth cruising down to Meglisalp. The settlement dates back to the Middle Ages of 1071. Grab a beer from their DIY trough-cooler out back.

Take It All In

Coasting along a rolling high traverse with a cliff below you and another above, the views across the valley are striking. Look down and back, and take in much of the day's run. Soon, the trail begins its 700m descent. In the final few hundred meters, choose between staying left to stop for celebratory beers at the Gasthaus Alpenrose, or heading right for the train and wherever your trail running shoes take you next.

Why We Love It

A friendly route where everyone greets in a variety of *Grüezi*, hello.

Alphorntreffen

Time your run for late June during the annual Seealpsee Alphorntreffen, or 'Meeting of the Alphorns'. Echoing alphorns will accompany you on your run!

Appenzellerland

Stop in Appenzell to see the folk art and colorfully painted frescoes on the buildings. Treat yourself to a *biberli*, a classic Swiss gingerbread.

Pro Tip 1

The Alpstein is a cobweb of interesting trails. This is a great area to customize your run and include a night at one of the many mountain huts.

Pro Tip 2

Stay in St. Gallen to enjoy the nightlife in the town's popular historic area before taking the train to Wasserauen. The entire trip is just an hour – and the second half features plenty of farms, rolling pastures, and herds of content cows.

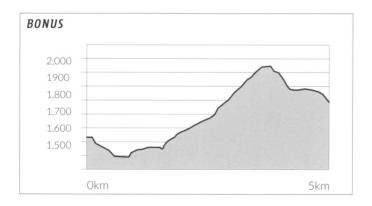

Bonus

For more running, once you reach Altenalp, traverse with a slight drop before turning back along the base of a wall with climbing routes. You'll rejoin the loop after passing through Schäfler and enjoying a bit of exposure, extending your run by 5km and 330m gain.

MAP

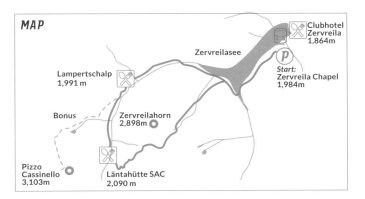

Clubhotel Zervreila 1,864m

Zervreilasee

Lampertschalp 1,991 m

Start: Zervreila Chapel 1,984m

Bonus

Zervreilahorn 2,898m

Pizzo Cassinello 3,103m

Läntahütte SAC 2,090 m

PROFILE

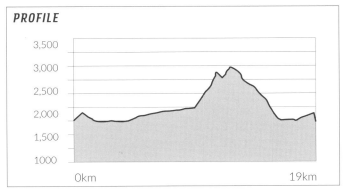

0km   19km

3,500
3,000
2,500
2,000
1,500
1000

DIFFICULTY

DISTANCE 19km
ASCENT 1,106m
HIGHEST POINT 2,712m

PEAK SPOTTING
- Zervreilahorn
- Piz Terri
- Güferhorn
- Rheinwaldhorn

STYLE
Flow 80%, Technical 20%

RUNNING
75%

CANTON
Graubünden

COURSE
Loop, counterclockwise

OTHER CHARACTERISTICS
- Cables / Ladders: No
- Social media hero: Yes

ACCESS
- Parking: Zervreila Chapel
- Bus: Vals, Zervreila

LET'S RUN!

Getting Started
Ringed by 3,000m peaks, the Zervreilahorn rises up from the end of the Valser Tal. While it appears to be a single pointed summit, it's actually a long serrated ridgeline. Starting beside the Zervreilasee, this run circles the prominent mountain.

A gently rolling dirt road along the Zevreilasee leads you deeper into the valley before fading into a flat grassy trail. Pass the barns at Lampertsch Alp, typical Vals farms roofed with stone-tiles, and continue speeding through the river plain towards Läntahütte. After nine fast and flat kilometers, you'll reach the Läntahütte, and just past it, the bridge to cross the Valser Rhein.

And Up
The climb begins on the other side of the river, where tight switchbacks lead up the steep trail. Alongside the spine of the Zervreilahorn, red and white paint directs your rock hopping to the high-point of the run, Furggelti.

That's a Wrap
The descent stretches out in front of you, following signs to Zervreila, and down to meet the same dirt road along the lake. Don't forget to look over your shoulder from time to time to admire the changing shape of the Zervreilahorn.

Why We Love It
Easy running, a rugged climb, circling a giant mohawk-like rock in a remote valley. What's not to love?

Not-to-be-Missed
Listen for snow cocks calling out from the rocky slopes of the Butzeggen.

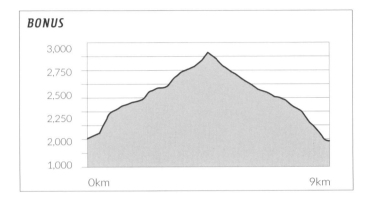

Bonus
A trip up to Pizzo Cassinello (3,103m) adds 9km and 1,138m gain if you want a bigger day. The trail to the summit splits just past Lampertsch Alp.

Pro Tip
Share the trail with two-wheeled traffic – a popular mountain bike trail connects Zervreila Lake to the Lampertsch Alp.

Valserwasser
Passing through Vals, you'll see the Valser mineral water company. Look closely at the label on a Valser water bottle and you'll see the Zervreilahorn.

Läntahütte
Built into an enormous rock, the tiny Läntahütte receives some of its supplies by helicopter, but is supplemented by fresh produce delivered by donkey. The hut serves regional specialties, has thirty-three beds, and a bouldering wall.

PIZ LANGUARD
PONTRESINA'S IBEX PARADISE

MAP

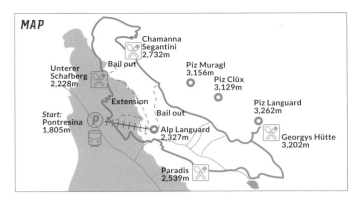

Chamanna
Segantini
2,732m

Bail out

Piz Muragl
3,156m

Piz Clüx
3,129m

Unterer
Schafberg
2,228m

Piz Languard
3,262m

Extension

Bail out

Georgys Hütte
3,202m

Start:
Pontresina
1,805m

Alp Languard
2,327m

Paradis
2,539m

PROFILE

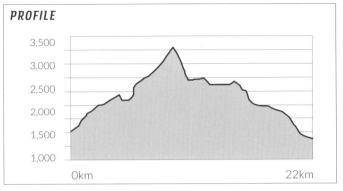

3,500
3,000
2,500
2,000
1,500
1,000

0km   22km

DIFFICULTY

DISTANCE   22km
ASCENT   1,620m
HIGHEST POINT   3,262m

PEAK SPOTTING
• Piz Bernina
• Piz Rosatsch
• Piz Corvatsch

PEAK TAGGING
• Piz Languard 3,262m

STYLE
Flow 80%, Technical 10%,
Exposed 10%

RUNNING
75%

CANTON
Graubünden

COURSE
Loop, counterclockwise

OTHER CHARACTERISTICS
• Cables / Ladders: No
• Social media hero: No

ACCESS
• Parking: Pontresina SPL
  lift station
• Train: Pontresina
• Lift / Bus: Pontresina to
  Alp Languard

LET'S RUN!

Getting Started
Most of the activity in Pontresina is centered along its long main street, Via Maistra. Our run starts at the southeast end of town, at the Pontresina SPL lift station. Head uphill to the Santa Maria Church past the remains of the five-sided Spaniola tower, built around 1200. You'll quickly leave the town behind as you climb through a beautiful forest, past brooks, breaking out into pastures and switchbacking to the ridgeline that leads to the Paradis Hut.

Up to the Steinbock Promenade
Coast down into the wide Val Languard, then over to Lej Languard. A short steep grunt over loose rock reminds you that almost all of today's run is over smooth, flowing trails. Enjoy the growing view, now including St. Moritz and other towns in the region. Look up to Piz Languard, and near the summit, you'll spot Georgy's hut – a chance to refuel.

To Georgy's and the Big Views
Gentle contours and flowy trails bring you to the summit push that switchbacks steeply up to Georgy's. Before or after a break at the hut, tackle the final climb to the summit of Piz Languard. It's short but steep. At 3,262m, it's your high point for the day with massive views in all directions!

Through the Avalanche Barriers
Back to the junction below the hut, the route contours along the slope, with gentle ups and downs past numerous avalanche barriers that protect Pontresina, far below. Rocky slopes (technical dancing required!) alternate with pleasant single-track in this section, and a final climb up to the Segantini hut, named for plein air Alpine painter Giovanni Segantini.

Kílian It

Gathering speed while dropping to town on flowy, classic Engadine trails, you might just feel like a pro. You'll contour on well-set flat stones around the corner, then switchback down a steep slope, later enjoying some sweet flat cruising along another round of flat paver stones. All of this fast running comes with big views of St. Moritz and the Pontresina Valley. You're looking right up Val Roseg, with a glimpse of the glacial Lej da Vadret, and Piz Corvatsch to your right.

Rest up at restaurant Unterer Schafberg if you like. There's more running on gentle downhill switchbacks, through pastures and woods, past ancient dry-set stone retaining walls and finally dropping to the pasture above town and back to your starting point.

Why We Love It
A high view-to-work ratio and great stops en route. Pontresina is a great place to finish the day or even stay for a long weekend!

Not-to-be-Missed
Pontresina-based trail runner and Olympian Julia Bleasdale recommends the fruit *Wähe*, or flan, made by Paradis hut's caretaker Pia. For thirty-five years, she's baked cakes at home each evening and then carried them up the next morning from Alp Languard. Pia is renowned throughout the valley so much so, that locals order in advance so they don't miss out!

Pro Tip 1
Bring your Engadine visitor card if you're staying at one of the hotels in the area. All the lifts will be free!

Pro Tip 2
This run may have the best distance-to-pie ratio of any run in this book. Choose wisely.

Extension
From the restaurant Unterer Schafberg, add on more flowy trails to lengthen your return to Pontresina. (See map).

Post-Run Zen
Drop in to the Santa Maria Church at the end of the run. It's considered to be one of the most important buildings in the entire canton and contains beautiful frescoes dating back eight centuries. Santa Maria Church also conveniently has parking and public bathrooms.

Welcome Home
Though native to the region, steinbock were reintroduced after being hunted to extirpation. A century ago, the Italian King Vittorio Emanuele III smuggled a few into Switzerland – all the ibex in the Alps share these few ancestors. The area around Piz Languard is home to 1,800 ibex, one of the largest colonies in the Alps. In the spring, the 'Kings of the Alps' seek fresh grass, and the entire herd wanders down to the edge of town!

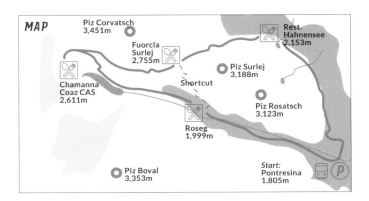

MAP

Piz Corvatsch 3,451m

Fuorcla Surlej 2,755m

Rest. Hahnensee 2,153m

Piz Surlej 3,188m

Chamanna Coaz CAS 2,611m

Shortcut

Piz Rosatsch 3,123m

Roseg 1,999m

Piz Boval 3,353m

Start: Pontresina 1,805m

PROFILE

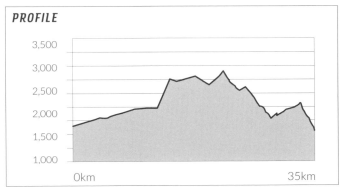

3,500
3,000
2,500
2,000
1,500
1,000

0km   35km

DIFFICULTY

DISTANCE	35km
ASCENT	1,655m
HIGHEST POINT	2,753m

PEAK SPOTTING
- Piz Morteratsch
- Piz Bernina
- Piz Roseg
- Piz Corvatsch
- Piz Rosatsch

STYLE
Flow 90%, Gritty 10%

RUNNING
75%

CANTON
Graubünden

COURSE
Loop, clockwise

OTHER CHARACTERISTICS
- Cables / Ladders: No
- Social media hero: Yes

ACCESS
- Parking: Pontresina Bahnhof
- Train: Pontresina

LET'S RUN!

Getting Started
This start couldn't be much easier! The Pontresina train station is 100m away from the trailhead. Pontresina, uphill, has everything you might need – a large super-market, gear stores, great cafes and restaurants, and hotels to extend your stay.

Stretch Your Legs
Start by cruising along the wide single-track, gently uphill towards the Val Roseg. You'll run along the river, a popular path with an interpretive trail. As you leave Pontresina, you're entering the wild Rosegtal, with sweeping views of your upcoming terrain.

Big Sky Country
Crossing the bridge before the Hotel and Restaurant Roseg Gletscher, the valley suddenly opens and you'll get big views of the flat, grassy Rosegtal and the moun-tains that ring it. Run past the inn along an old farm road, past chalets, and up the valley winding your way through grazing herds of cows, ending with running over old glacial moraines as you twist and turn your way up to Lej da Vadret.

Up to Coaz
With the first 12km run being relatively flat, you've reached the end of the valley. Enjoy a break at the wild-feeling Lej da Vadret, well-known for its plentiful alpine flowers. Until recent recession, the glacier calved ice directly into the lake. The steep trail towards the Coaz hut is sure to slow your pace so buckle down for a fast hike up. The angle lessens before long, rocky single-track segues to dirt and pasture, and you'll be at the junction for Chamanna Coaz. Head left for a short flat cruise and a break at a classic Swiss Alpine Club hut!

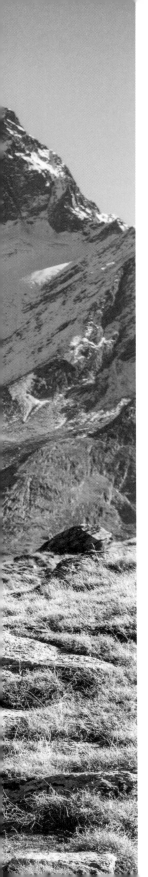

The High Country

Done with your torte and coffee? It's time to jog uphill through alpine pastures, with occasional diversions for side paths. You'll get glimpses of Lej da Vadret below and big views of Morteratsch, Bernina on the Italian border, and Roseg. Slightly more technical running and a final push lead to Fuorcla Surlej and views towards St. Moritz and Silvaplana, and the stone Berghaus – the high-point for the day. Stop in for self-service meals, and be sure to say hi to the friendly hut dog, Janis.

A New View

Over the col, it's time to enjoy a long coast through pastures with completely new views. As you cruise through the ski terrain of Murtel ski station, you'll see Lej Silvaplauna and Lej Segl at your feet. The route contours around a broad slope of Munt Arlas before descending to Lej dals Chöds. Beyond Bergrestaurant Hahnensee, you'll continue descending to a trail junction at a low point.

Gentle climbing brings back the sweat, but you won't notice it – the running is close to perfect here on wooded trail. The day finishes with single-track bliss, as you weave through the forest, finishing in town near the train station.

Why We Love It

Easy cruising through a dramatic valley with big views, and a second half that's easy coasting through beautiful forests.

Refuel by the Centimeter

Take the side trail to the Swiss Alpine Club's old-school hut, Chamanna Coaz that sells cake and torte by the centimeter. Order and watch some precision measurement in action! Cost: 1.50 CHF per centimeter.

Rest or Run

You'll have another nice opportunity for a break at Bergrestaurant Hahnensee, beside Lej dals Chöds. There's water available, as well as a full menu, too. We recommend the *Älplermagronen* and *Engadiner Nusstorte.*

Bonus

Not ready for the run to end? Turn at the junction for Muottas da Schlaringa. Just ten minutes away, you'll take in views of St. Moritz, the lakes in the region, the village of Celerina, and Pontresina. There's even a great view through Berninapass directly at the dramatic Piz dal Teo.

Cheers

Rehydrate with some beers at the modern but cozy Gianottis in town.

MAP

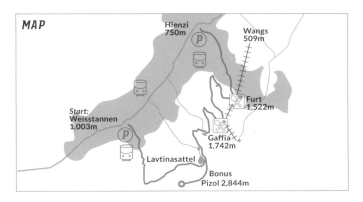

Hienzi 750m

Wangs 509m

Furt 1,522m

Start: Weisstannen 1,003m

Gaffia 1,742m

Lavtinasattel

Bonus Pizol 2,844m

PROFILE

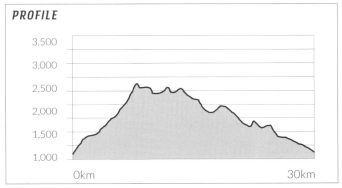

3,500
3,000
2,500
2,000
1,500
1,000

0km   30km

DIFFICULTY

DISTANCE   30km
ASCENT   2,272m
HIGHEST POINT   2,570m

PEAK SPOTTING
- Pizol
- Hangsackgrot
- Alvier

STYLE
Flow 80%, Technical 20%

RUNNING
75%

CANTON
St. Gallen

COURSE
Point to point

OTHER CHARACTERISTICS
- Cables / Ladders: No
- Social media hero: No

ACCESS
- Parking: Weisstannental, Mels or Hienzi
- Bus: Weisstannen Oberdorf
- Lift: Gaffia or Furt

LET'S RUN!

Getting Started
A stone's throw from Liechtenstein on Switzerland's east border lies the remote Weisstannental. Getting there can be an effort, but the payoff is worth it. You'll start the day at Weisstannen. Fill up at the fountain in the village center, and if you need it, grab some breakfast at the Hotel Gemse.

Whether you've arrived by car or public transport, head along the river, past a farm, hopping across the Gufelbach on an old bridge, and warm up with a fast hike up the steep one-lane road. Reaching a wide-open pasture, you can break into a run to the end of the valley. When you find yourself surrounded by steep walls at Batöni, join hiking tour 73, Switzerland's 100km long Sardona-Welterbe-Weg.

Steinbocks, Chamois and Eagles
Head left and get serious about gaining vertical. Airy twists and turns take you into an enormous basin, past the solitary Stofel cabin, and to a reliable cistern with water at Under Läger. Domestic and wild animals share the basin with cows on our side and steinbock on the wilder slopes to the east. Gentle uphill through the pasture leads to a series of switchbacks that complete the 1,500m push to today's high-point, Lavtinasattel. Take a break and take in the views. Enjoy the solitude of the col, as you're about to join one of Switzerland's more popular day hikes.

Twisting Around the Tarns
Ready for that reward? Here come the lakes. Dance along technical alpine terrain, contour around Wildsee, then switchback your way down to Schottensee, 100m below. Time to log some kilometers, dodging tourists along long switchbacks and up a broad, grassy ridge to one of the best 360-degree views of the day. Gaze out to the Graubünden region, beyond Sargans into Liechtenstein, to Austria, and north to the Alpstein.

Grateful for Gaffia

Sweet, slightly technical running leads down and past Schwarzsee, and in a few minutes you're at yet another big view at Rossstall. Did we mention the views were incredible on today's run? In sight: Lake Constance on the German border, the Glarus mountains, and the Grison Alps to the south.

One of today's speediest sections is still ahead. Cruise down and drop off the ridge, running around the next lake, Baschalva. Leaping into a technical downhill, remember to hit the brakes at Gaffia, where you'll find water, restaurant choices and an option to spare yourself the knee pounding with cable transport down to Wangs.

See What the Crowds are Missing

Good news: a quiet return! You'll contour above and below precipices, climbing 100m to a grassy high-point at Garmil with an expansive view of dozens of peaks and three valleys below. Relax and let your legs go! There's dirt-filled super-fast cruising on long switchbacks through pastures and woods. A faint section of new trail (watch carefully!) leads to a wooded downhill. Finally, a combination of road and short trail sections wind down to Hienzi where a cold trough awaits.

Why We Love It
The work comes early... and after that, it's nearly all downhill, coasting around alpine tarns and along broad, windswept ridges.

Not-to-be-Missed
Soaking in the views at Lavtinasattel.

Pro Tip
Run this route during the hottest days of the summer, and plan for an ice-cold dip. There's no shortage of lakes to choose from! Running the route in early fall or late spring? Bring traction – snow lingers on the slopes of the high pass, making running tricky at best.

Tag Pizol
Pizol is the highest mountain entirely contained within the St. Gallen canton. If you want to get a little higher, head up to the 2,844m summit as a bonus. The up-and-back adds 3.5km and 410m to the route.

Shifting Plates
Today's run takes place in the Sardona Tectonic Area, a Unesco World Heritage Site where the mountain formation process and plate tectonics can be viewed up close. Watch for interpretive panels along the route.

Logistics
Don't forget to factor in bus travel for the beginning or end of your run. Our suggestion – park at the finish. It's nice to see your car waiting for you at Hienzi, and you won't have to worry about missing the last Postbus! Feeling hardcore? You can always skip the bus and run a bonus 7km along the river between Weisstannen and Hienzi.

Ride Down
The lifts at Gaffia or Furt provide a more mellow way to end the day if you'd rather skip some pavement ahead and avoid roads, instead ending your day at Wangs.

Come Back with a Bike
Much of today's route includes sections of the Pizol Challenge, a popular 21km mountain bike tour.

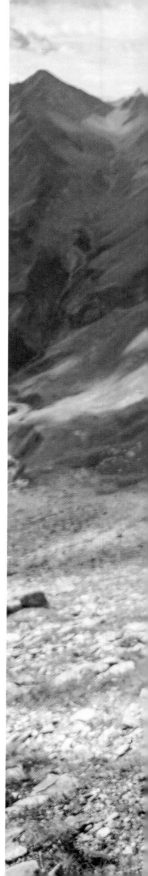

THE MAKING OF

5
ROLLED ANKLES

10
PAIRS OF SHOES
DESTROYED

0
BLISTERS

PHOTOS
MADE: 50,000
KEPT: 3,500

13:18
LONGEST DAY
ON THE TRAIL

4
TRAIL-BUTTER
SHIPMENTS FROM U.S.

SUNSETS
NOT NEARLY ENOUGH, BUT
MORE THAN ENOUGH
CLOUDY EVENINGS

LOST TRACK
GAS STATION DINNERS
ON THE DRIVE HOME

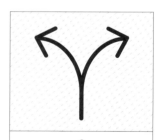

8
NEW ROUTES TRIED
BUT DID NOT MAKE THE CUT

BIGGEST SURPRISE
HOW FEW PEOPLE WE
ACTUALLY SAW ON OUR
ROUTES

VERTICAL GAIN IN 2017
APPROX 6,500KM AND
350,000M – WELCOME
TO THE SWISS ALPS

KICK ASS ROUTES
JANINE CREATED FIVE
THAT KICKED HER ASS – NO
COMMENT AS TO WHICH ONES

NEW NICKNAMES

JANINE
BECAME BOTH
'ADD ON' FOR HER
CEASELESS DESIRE TO
KEEP DOING JUST THAT
ON SO MANY TOURS.
AS WELL AS 'DIESEL'
FOR CONTINUING TO
GRIND ALONG WHEN
EVERYONE ELSE WAS
CURSING HER DAMNED
ADD ONS

FAVOURITE TRAILS

JANINE:
LAC DE MOIRY

DAN:
ZERMATT,
HARDERGRAT,
MONTE ZUCCHERO

DOUG:
STECHELBERG-KANDERSTEG

KIM:
JAZZILÜCKE LOOP,
SIMPLON

AND NOW COMES THE FUN PART...